Happiness
at the

13 Powerful Strategies For Finding
Happiness At Home And On The Job

By Jim Smith, PCC
The Executive Happiness Coach®

HSOL Press

Remember to
STAND TALL.
BREATHE DEEPLY.
SMILE Often!

Jim Smith
'09

HSOL Press
6432 Nelwood Rd
Cleveland, OH 44130-3211

This material was created and is owned by
Jim Smith, The Executive Happiness Coach®.

Cover and book design by Black Cat Creative Services, Cleveland, OH
Manufactured in the United States of America

10   9   8   7   6   5   4   3   2   1

Library of Congress Cataloging-in-Publication Data

Smith, Jim
Happiness at the speed of life: 13 powerful strategies for finding happiness at
home and on the job / Jim Smith
    p. cm.

1. Happiness. 2. Self-Improvement
Includes endnotes and bibliographical references

ISBN: 978-0-615-28942-7

Library of Congress Control Number: 2009925935

Dedication:

To those who have left this world and moved to the spiritual plane, I dedicate this book. Though you are gone, the lessons you left with me stay with me always.

Sean Torrance Smith, my little brother who lived life full out and at the Speed of Life, even after receiving a death sentence from cancer at age 24. You taught me that Attitude is, indeed, a choice.

Ann Marilyn Dunning, my dear mother-in-law for 30 years, who battled Multiple Sclerosis for 50 years and who modeled unconditional Love, always. You taught me how to live life with great Joy and Happiness even in the presence of pain and disability.

Kara Watsana Angela Smith, my Thai beauty and adopted daughter, who came to our family late and left us far too early. You showed me how to live fully in the present, and taught me that what happened in the past does not matter as long as the future is bright.

~~☺~~☺~~☺~~☺~~

Contents:

Foreword

"It's not enough to have lived. We should be determined to live for something. May I suggest that it be creating joy for others, sharing what we have for the betterment of personkind, bringing hope to the lost and love to the lonely."

—Leo F. Buscaglia, 1924–1998

"An Unexamined Life is not worth living."

—Socrates, 470–399 BCE

I'd like to invite you to take a walk with me. On this journey you'll learn that Happiness is within all of us, if we choose to be open to it. You'll get to know me, my family, some of my clients, and learn about my business—helping others understand how living with happiness everyday makes their lives richer, healthier, and more satisfying.

This book is not about adopting a Pollyanna view of life. What I'll share is my story; a story full of challenges, frustrations, and even heart-wrenching tragedies—the things we all experience in our lives. By focusing on happiness, choosing it as our basic attitude, we will be better able to appreciate the ups and survive the downs of everyday life. My mantra—Happiness is a decision, not an event—teaches us that we are in control of our responses to life's daily pressures. Happiness is not something that will come tomorrow; we must choose it today.

In each section of the book, you will learn about one of the *13 Principles of Happiness*, see how I have experienced it in my life, discover how it can be applied in your life and your work place, and learn about some fun and interesting resources related to that principle.

Now, it's time to stand tall, take a deep breath, smile... **and take a walk with me.**

—Jim Smith, The Executive Happiness Coach®

~~☺~~☺~~☺~~☺~~

How To Read This Book

While this book aims to help you experience more happiness in your life, it is not a step-by-step "how-to manual" on how to be a happier person. I do not offer a happiness pyramid, quadrant model, or Venn diagram to guide you on your quest. Rather, herein are lessons about *The 13 Principles of Happiness* wrapped around short essays, personal reflections, and stories about experiences others or I have had. Woven in you'll find lessons, tips, tools, and ideas for application in your personal life and in the workplace, and even some random websites or web tools that have no purpose except to bring you a smile....

As you read, you will find various icons identifying what I am sharing: a personal reflection, tips & tools, application for the workplace, or random happiness activity. These are the icons you'll see:

| Personal Reflection | Tips & Tools | Happiness @ Work | Random Happiness |

The intent of this book is to give you insights on how you can bring more happiness into your life. There is work to be done; yet the power to be a happier person is within you. These essays, reflections, and stories are each connected to one of *The 13 Principles of Happiness*, which they also seek to explain. It is through the adoption of these principles that I believe you can learn to become a happier, more appreciative, person.

Website Resources

Throughout the book you will find websites that take you to other Happiness resources or refer to resources on my own website. Reading this book at the beach or in a place with no Internet access? No worries, my dear reader—and no need to book mark those pages, either. You will find all website references, in the order they appear in the book, in the Appendix. So relax and enjoy your reading. You can surf the web later.

Final Note On Reading This Book

As you read about *The 13 Principles of Happiness*, some of them will seem very comfortable and familiar to you; you will say, "I already do that." Some principles may feel more challenging, while others may feel out of reach for you right now. Nevertheless, if you are trying to achieve more happiness in your life, start working with the principles that seem more comfortable and more achievable for you. As you build your happiness skills, the others will become less challenging.

Enjoy the Journey...

Introduction

The Power Of "Positive" Emotion

In 2003, I began a six-month class developed and taught by Martin Seligman, PhD, one of the creators of modern Positive Psychology. Traditional psychology, rooted in the theories of Sigmund Freud and Carl Jung, focuses on fixing the mental and emotional issues causing dysfunction in people's lives—helping them to get their lives back to a "normal" state. Seligman and his colleagues asked, "If we can help dysfunctional people move to a more neutral condition, is there something we can do to help functional people create a better condition?" They studied the cause-and-effect cycle of POSITIVE emotions, e.g., gratitude, joy, hope, interest, contentment, love, and, of course, happiness. They sought to develop a disciplined approach "to make normal life more fulfilling."[1]

Their findings revealed some amazing things—specifically, people who experience more positive emotion in their lives...

- *Are more resilient.* They hold up to stress better and recover from negative or traumatic situations more quickly.

- *Are more creative.* They typically see more options available to them and are more comfortable trying new ideas and experiences.

- *Are healthier.* The mind-body connection is strong. In clinical studies, researchers found that people who were trained to focus on and write about the positive aspects of their lives had more rapid cardiovascular recovery from stressful events than both the negative-focus group and the neutral (control) group.

- *Live longer.* Several long-term studies link positive emotion to longer life. One of these is the Nun Study: 678 Notre Dame sisters (survivors aged 75 to 100+) participating in longevity research. Researchers analyzed autobiographies written by the nuns upon joining the order in their early 20s. Looking for key words such as "happy," "joy," "love," "hopeful" and "content," they found that nuns who articulated more positive emotions in their early lives, lived as much as 10-years longer and had lower rates of Alzheimer's than those expressing fewer positive emotions.[2]

The best news to emerge from the research is that people—including YOU—can learn to experience more positive emotions in their life by engaging in a variety of reflective, skill-building exercises.

Train Your Emotions

It's a generally accepted truth that the path to better physical health includes diet and exercise. We know we must pay attention to the foods we eat and work our bodies if we want to feel good.

For overall health, we must also attend to our emotional "muscles." For just as our legs and arms grow stronger when we work out, so do our moods and emotions grow stronger the more often they are exercised.

Unfortunately for many of us, we exercise our worry, anxiety, and fear muscles every day, so they are quite strong. If we want to experience more joy and happiness in our life, we must consciously practice these emotional states every day so that, when we are under stress, our positive emotional muscles are strong enough to pull us through.

Let me be clear: Being *happy* does not mean being bubbly, smiling, and carefree all the time, nor does it imply the constant pursuit of pleasure and feel-good activities. Positive emotion can show up in very quiet ways in our lives, such as feeling hopeful, noticing things we are grateful for, appreciating the beauty that exists in everyday life, or simply being content and at peace. Our media-drenched culture tends to focus on what is bizarre and negative, yet there is so much to enjoy when we shift the lens we use to look at the world.

This book is about taking a different approach to your life, and to finding, building, and maintaining your "Happiness muscles" in new and practical ways.

~~☺~~☺~~☺~~☺~~

An example of the Tips Lists you'll find throughout the book

Tips for Training Your Positive Emotion Muscles

Are you ready to give your emotional muscles their first workout? Here are three exercises to get you started. These exercises are a sampling of what's in store for you throughout the book. You'll find many other exercises and daily practices to strengthen your "positive emotion muscles!" as you read on.

Document Your Blessings. At the end of each day, write down three things that went really well that day. These may range from simple (a friend bought me coffee this morning) to really big (I got a promotion!). Next to each blessing, answer the question: "Why did this good thing happen?" Try this for 30 days, and notice how it increases your daily awareness of the good things that occur in your life.

Some may find this difficult to do at first. That's a sign your "positive awareness" muscle is a bit weaker. If so, start with one blessing per day; you'll find the muscle strengthens over time (see more on this exercise in Chapter 3, Principle 9: Pay Attention).

Take a "Beauty Walk." Give yourself 20–30 minutes for this activity. Take a relaxed walk around your neighborhood, office complex, or even the local mall—it's best if you choose a location you are familiar with. As you walk, invite yourself to notice the world differently, through a *positive* lens. Focus your attention on things you don't normally notice: the splash of color on those hydrangea bushes up the street; the neighbor cutting the lawn of an elderly widow; toddlers in awe of the leaping water in a mall fountain; wildflowers growing in the cracks of a driveway; the gentle song of a wind chime. For extra impact, take time to write it all down, or tell the "story" of your walk to a friend, and notice how savoring the experience through retelling it heightens your positive feelings.

Write a Gratitude Letter. Gratitude, a positive emotion, connects us to the kindness of others—yet our society lacks many formal rituals for thanking others. Think of someone from your past who has made a difference for you by their kindness, but who has never heard you express your gratitude. Write them a letter, expressing in concrete, specific terms what they did for you, how it affected your life, and how you are grateful to them. Make it heartfelt. For extra impact, deliver it personally and read it aloud in their presence.

Many of us spend half or more of our waking hours on the job, so it is just as important to experience Happiness in the workplace as in our personal life. That's what I explore in the Happiness @work segments.

Training Emotions In The Workplace

When under the gun, understaffed due to vacations, in the midst of a dozen conflicting priorities, and feeling like you are being "meeting'd" to death, it can be tough to practice optimism.
Though some corporate cultures teach that action "off the agenda" is a mortal sin, we know that taking a moment to just *be* can help us re-center and return to the workplace with more energy and creativity.

Try this to start out your next team or executive staff meeting, it's an exercise I call, simply, **Good News.**

Instructions: As the meeting starts, announce that you're going to begin by going around and asking everyone to share some Good News from the past week. It can be personal or workplace focused. Be sure to have something of your own to start! Not only might you learn a thing or two about how others on your team think, but be prepared to watch the group's energy rise a notch or three as people share things that they are happy or proud about.

Variation: At the end of a meeting, ask everyone to identify something positive they are taking away from the meeting. Either version of this exercise will help the entire group strengthen their positive emotion muscles.

Many of the stories I relate in this book deal with workplace issues and the challenges faced by business leaders. In my three decades of corporate experience, I've come to realize that the role of a leader is not the sole property of those who sit in offices with doors. Leaders are all around—at the reception desk, in the copy room, in the back offices and in the cubicles that fill the internal spaces. Leadership is an attitude; it's a mind set focused on providing a vision for others, supporting them in their growth, and serving as a positive role model.

I will repeat this concept many times in the book. I believe that in order to truly have a happier life you must be balanced in your home and work life. Enlightened leaders will work to gauge and build the happiness levels of their employees. But this is not just about presidents, VPs, managers, and others with executive titles. It's also about you—the human being—and how you show up.

So remember...

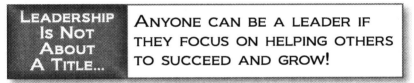

LEADERSHIP Is Not About A Title... ANYONE CAN BE A LEADER IF THEY FOCUS ON HELPING OTHERS TO SUCCEED AND GROW!

~~☺~~☺~~☺~~☺~~

Finally, I share personal reflections on how I see happiness show up in my life – and invite you to notice how it does the same in yours.

Lessons From The Beach

I take an annual beach vacation. The combination of sun, sand, sea, and the occasional spectacular storm creates a perfect setting for detachment. Every day is pretty much the same, so it's easy to slip into a relaxed state of observation. During one trip a few years ago, when I'd forgotten about doing work and was focused on just BEING, I began to record my observations in my journal—pages and pages of them. What emerged was both fun and interesting, here are just a few of them. As you read, think of these as metaphors for life and happiness.

Riding Jet Skis

~ The faster you are going when you take your foot off the gas, the farther your momentum carries you before you come to a complete stop.

~ Being dumped and getting wet are part of the fun.

~ Before you leave the dock, learn how to right the boat in case you flip.

Golf

~ Golfers don't care about weather. When playing a match, everyone has to deal with the same conditions. The playing field is always level.

The Beach

~ Stormy seas make for the best body surfing.

~ What looks like a pitch-black night from inside a lit house is a starlit night out on the beach. But you don't know that until you venture out and let your eyes adjust.

~ Dark clouds and thunder don't necessarily mean that it's going to rain; and sunshine doesn't mean that it won't.

~ The sands shift overnight, every night. Unless your trail is deep and strong it won't be there tomorrow.

~ The winds can change at any time and can come from multiple directions even in the same day. If your umbrella is not firmly rooted, it gets blown away.

~ Cloudy days can be a blessing.

~ Know your own limits or you will ruin the fun.

~ Afternoon naps are a delightful decadence.

Questions for you:

What are YOUR life metaphors? What meaning do they hold for you?

If you notice your metaphors pull you down, consider replacing them with stories that engage you rather than depress you.

~~☺~~☺~~☺~~☺~~

—Chapter 1—

The 13 Principles Of Happiness

Since 2003, The 13 Principles of Happiness have hung on bulletin boards, cubicle walls, refrigerators, and bathroom mirrors, and have inspired parents, teens, coworkers, and thousands of online readers.

1. *Become Positively Self-ish*

   When you take care of yourself first, you build a foundation for stronger relationships with others, increase your capacity, and reduce doubt.

2. *Live Your Values*

   Clearly identify and proclaim your personal values through the way you live and work. You are more likely to spot opportunities when you know what they look like.

3. *Live for Life, not Stuff*

   Let go of possessions, roles, lifestyles that others and a marketing-hyped society impose on you; focus instead on what truly brings you Joy.

4. *Be Early*

   Whether it is project deadlines, appointments, or learning opportunities, get there before you are expected, and watch your stress load decrease exponentially.

5. *Build Reserves*

   Identify what worries you, and work to create extra in your life, whether that is money, personal space, or extra toilet paper in the cabinet.

6. *Tolerate Nothing*

   Continually identify and eliminate all the little "stuff" which causes you friction and drains your energy.

7. *Choose to Respond*

   What happens is going to happen, regardless. Accept constant, discontinuous change as reality and instead of reacting, respond with curiosity.

8. *Stimulate Your Development*

   Surround yourself with environments and people that continually challenge you, energize you, and literally pull you forward. Have adventures.

9. *Pay Attention*

When we are on autopilot, life just happens around us. Look. Listen. Notice. The sunset in your own backyard can be just as wondrous as the one at the beach.

10. *Simplify*

Automate, delegate, or eliminate tasks or goals that complicate your life. Being content with simpler pleasures increases your opportunity for awe.

11. *Speak the Truth*

Stop playing games. Recognize that though the truth may sometimes sting, it is the starting place for all progress. Challenge others to see the truth.

12. *Focus on Today*

Waiting for something to happen "tomorrow" in order for you to be happy is like watching yourself in the mirror and saying "You go first."

13. *Be Authentic*

Be yourself, not somebody else.

**Happiness is a mode of travel,
not a destination.**

Enjoy the ride.

For a full-color copy of The 13 Principles of Happiness suitable for framing or posting, go to http://tinyurl.com/Happiness13

~~☺~~☺~~☺~~☺~~

Building On The Four Foundations

The 13 Principles of Happiness are organized into four Foundational concepts. In chapters 2 through 5 we will examine each concept and its supporting Principles. Here's a preview:

1. *Take Your Own Oxygen First* — Keeping your oxygen tank on "full" increases your capacity for working with others. You feel stronger and more balanced as you deal with life's concerns, rather than feeling empty or overwhelmed.

Supporting Happiness Principles:
1. Become Positively Self-ish
2. Live Your Values
3. Live for Life, not Stuff

2. *Identify And Eliminate The Frictions In Your Life* — Frictions slow you down, drain your energy, and use up the available "psychic RAM" in your brain. When you eliminate frictions, you free your capacity for other opportunities. With fewer frictions, your life is easier; you live in more of a "flow" state, you reduce your feelings of stress, and you feel better, physically, mentally, emotionally, and spiritually.

Supporting Happiness Principles:
4. Be Early
5. Build Reserves
6. Tolerate Nothing

3. *Notice And Use Your Power To Choose* — You hold the power to control significant portions of your life. When you learn to access your power, your life shifts: you are rarely a victim, change is easier for you, and fewer issues appear as obstacles, since you clearly understand that even when you do not like the trip, you can choose the route. From a place of choice, it is easier to make decisions about your life.

Supporting Happiness Principles:
7. Choose to Respond
8. Stimulate Your Development
9. Pay Attention
10. Simplify

4. *Be, Boldly, The Real You* — When you learn to be more "comfortable in your own skin," you find it easier to live fully in the moment. Your priorities are clear, you let go of needing the future to be a particular way, and you are more present to enjoy what IS to the fullest. Because you fear less, you are far more comfortable respecting others' values; and others are more likely to want to hang around with you because you are happier.

Supporting Happiness Principles:
11. Speak the Truth
12. Focus on Today
13. Be Authentic

—Chapter 2—

Take Your Own Oxygen First

Principle #1.   Become Positively Self-ish

Principle #2.   Live Your Values

Principle #3.   Live for Life, Not Stuff

If you've ever traveled on a plane you are probably familiar with the mandatory safety talk delivered by your flight crew just prior to takeoff. After pointing out the location of the emergency exits and explaining how to use of seat belts, they say:

> *"In the unlikely event of a loss of cabin pressure, oxygen masks will drop from the overhead compartment <....> If you are traveling with a small child or someone who needs assistance, put on your own mask before helping others with theirs."*

Many of us react to these instructions as if we have been told to cross the street with our eyes closed. It goes against our instincts not to help the people we are with first and then take care of ourselves. What about my kids/spouse/ friend/grandma? How can I take my own oxygen first when they need me?

Hey, if you're not breathing, you'll be of little use to them during the rest of the trip. Things that may at first seem like selfish acts can, in fact, expand your capacity to take care of others—and I call that being "positively self-ish."

Taking your own oxygen first also means attending to your own infrastructure—making sure you understand and honor your personal values and know what is truly important to you.

~~☺~~☺~~☺~~☺~~

Happiness ❶ Principle

Be Positively Self-ish

When you take care of yourself first, you build a foundation for stronger relationships with others, increase your capacity, and reduce doubt.

We live in a time of constant, discontinuous change, overbooked schedules, and multiple conflicting demands on our time and resources. To manage our lives effectively, we need to keep our energy reserves high. To do this, we each need to practice a little selfishness.

By selfishness I don't mean refusing to share your toys, hiding the last few cookies so no one else eats them, or generally thinking only of yourself. In this context, the selfishness I am speaking about is thinking *first* of your own needs because you understand that when you do, you have more capacity to be there for others. It is about identifying what you need in order to function at peak effectiveness, and making sure you get it for yourself. Finally, it is about accepting responsibility for your own happiness instead of waiting for someone or something else to "make" you happy. So, how can you practice positively self-ish behavior? Here are a few tips.

Create "Me Time." Me Time is the space set aside to nurture your own balance and happiness. Block time on your schedule each week to do something you like to do, something that refills your tank. It might be an activity that involves someone else or it may be simple and solitary, like reading a book or taking a hot bath without being interrupted. If you currently spend zero time on such activities, then even five minutes a day may be sufficient to refuel. Actually scheduling it dramatically increases the probability it will happen.

Let Go of Guilt over putting yourself first. A credo I live by goes like this: "The secret to raising happy kids is to first have a happy marriage." The corollary to that is: "The secret to having happy relationships is to first be happy yourself." When you focus on your own needs first, you are creating a solid foundation that will benefit all the other significant players in your life.

Say No. Legitimate obligations and responsibilities deserve your attention. But not every request for your time falls into that category. Give yourself permission to decline invitations to events you really don't want to attend or which will stress you. Say no "selfishly" to additional responsibility if that's what feels right.

To help you determine what deserves a 'No', you might create a checklist based on your personal values to sort out what is truly important (see Values exercise in the next section, Principle 2).

Disconnect From Other's Expectations. What about that professional association, volunteer organization, or church group you belong to because it's the "right thing to do" even though the leadership is ineffective or the programs are off-target for you? Ask them to take your name off their list.

Protect Your Priorities. A busy schedule places extra demands on you. Resist the urge to skip your workout or give up sleep in order to create more time. Work with others to schedule around YOUR priorities. When you do show up, you'll be able to contribute more, avoid resentment, and be happier.

Creating Memories

 I am a huge fan of *The Lord Of The Rings* stories going back over 30 years and dozens of readings, including to my children as a bedtime story. I loved Peter Jackson's interpretation of the story in his 2001 movie "The Fellowship of the Ring". And so, when my then-17-year-old son invited me to attend a midnight premiere of "The Two Towers" (part two of the trilogy), I said, "Oh, Yes!" on impulse.

As the date approached, I began to rethink my decision. I'm a *very* busy guy, juggling my business with teaching, family time, and volunteer work. Was I *crazy*, thinking I could stay up till 4AM when I was running a big volunteer event the next day? Wasn't it irresponsible of me to lose so much sleep? Middle-aged fathers of four don't do this sort of thing. How silly!

The evening of the movie premiere arrived, and I still had much to do for the next day. It was insane to drop it all and take a nap so I could get up and head out at 11PM with my son. I thought of at least two-dozen reasons why I should skip the movie.

But then I stepped back and looked at my decision. Did I really want to go? *Yes*. Were there numerous logical reasons why I should just stay home and go to bed? *OK, yes*. Was I hurting anyone by going to the midnight show? *Well, no*. Which choice would make me happier? *Going to the show*.

So I did the selfish thing. I took my three decades of pent-up excitement to the theater and stood in line with (literally) a thousand high school and college kids to see that movie the first possible second I could. I was one of less than a dozen adults in three filled-to-capacity theaters. I allowed myself three wonderful hours to be enthralled with the reenactment of Part 2 of my all-time favorite book.

And you know what? The next morning I was tired and a bit crabby, and I snapped at my wife a few times as she rushed me through getting ready at the last minute; and she forgave me. At the end of the day, I was SO happy that I had allowed myself that little indulgence—really happy. For the rest of my days, that happiness is mine to cherish. Sitting with my son in a packed theater at 3 AM, creating a memory, and sharing an experience together— because I didn't listen to logic, but instead was positively selfish.

Pumping Self-Serve Gas

One of the jobs of a leader is to get things done through other people — to delegate tasks and decisions. We've all been taught that recognizing and rewarding the performance of our people will "keep their gas tanks on Full" and their performance high. Great wisdom that works, but that essentially puts you in the role of Gas Pump Attendant. What if you could institute Self-Serve? Teach your people and give them permission to be selfish, and you'll empower them to refuel at will. Your people will be happier and you'll increase your impact as a leader.

A Self-Serve Exercise. Give everyone on your team a dozen large gold foil stars at the beginning of the month. Hang one or two large pieces of flip-chart paper on a wall in a high-traffic area. Draw an enormous star on it (big enough to accommodate all the gold foil stars). Tell everyone they are to use their gold stars to recognize coworkers for doing something great during the next month, like serving a client, helping a coworker, solving a problem. When they award the star, have them write the person's name and the date on the star with permanent marker, and deliver it personally to that coworker at your team's next morning or weekly meeting, and explain why they are awarding this star. The recipients then post their stars on the giant star poster. All allocated stars must be spent before the end of the month. Here's a twist: Give everyone permission to award one of the stars to themselves.

When the big star gets filled, hold a little celebration (even a pot luck, if funds are tight) and spend a few minutes reviewing all the reasons people appreciated one another. Watch what happens when you empower people and allow them to be just a little selfish...

So remember...

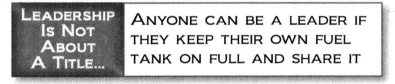

LEADERSHIP IS NOT ABOUT A TITLE... ANYONE CAN BE A LEADER IF THEY KEEP THEIR OWN FUEL TANK ON FULL AND SHARE IT

~~☺~~☺~~☺~~☺~~

Happiness By The Numbers

This University of Pennsylvania website http://www.authentichappiness.com hosts all the happiness assessments created by Martin Seligman, PhD, the father of Positive Psychology (and also my lead instructor during my Authentic Happiness® Coach certification training). You can register to create an account, and then explore the many tools in the Testing Center. Some take 30 seconds, others 25 minutes.

The assessments measure character strengths and aspects of happiness. All are yours to use at no charge. For each one, you'll immediately receive your score and see how it compares to the thousands of others who have visited this website. The site stores your scores, so that you can return later and see how far you've progressed (I have records at the site back to 2001!), or to check in on your current emotional state.

~~☺~~☺~~☺~~☺~~

Happiness ② Principle

Live Your Values

Whenever I lead a program that addresses values, I begin by asking, "Who in this room has a clearly defined set of core values?" Typically, two-thirds of the hands in the room might go up. "Not that I want to disagree with my audience," I continue, "but those of you who did not raise their hands are incorrect in thinking you don't have a set of personal values—you do!" At this, heads in the audience begin to nod and eyebrows go up as the concept sinks in.

Whether we can articulate them clearly or not, we all operate from a base of beliefs that guide our lives. Those things we hold to be true for ourselves are our core values.

What's the value of Values? Our values serve as the framework upon which we build our lives as well as the "filter" through which we view and relate to the rest of the world. When we behave in alignment with our values, our framework feels solid and our view of the world is positive. When what we say and what we do are not in sync—when we don't Live those Values—we feel out of alignment and, ultimately, unhappy.

When we proclaim our values to ourselves and to the world, and then behave in accord with those values, we experience more joy, peace, and contentment in our lives. We feel more in harmony with ourselves. We are more likely to notice opportunities in our life that support our values. And in the end we are happier.

How do we live our Values? Start by writing them out. When you write your values, they become more real.**

Your first draft may not feel complete; not to worry, live with the document for a few weeks, then return and edit until the values ring true for you. You might begin with simple terms like "Friendship" and edit your way to define that as, "I make time in my life to build deeper relationships with the people I care about."

**Visit my website for a short exercise to help you select and prioritize your values: http://www.theexecutivehappinesscoach.com/resources/values.pdf

Other ways you can Live Your Values:

Use them to "re-center" yourself. Whenever you feel unhappy or out-of-balance, pull out your list and ask, "In what ways am I disconnected from my core values?" Make a list if you need to, then take action to change that condition(s).

Share your list of values with others. Your behavior will make more sense when others understand the logic behind what you do. For example, if you share with others that you value Family and being present at family events, they may be more tolerant when you ask for a two-hour lunch to attend the school play.

Review them regularly. Spend fifteen minutes at the start or end of every week to review your values and remind yourself what's most important to you. You will notice your decisions become easier when you "own" your values completely and let them guide you.

Remember: Values are what we hold to be true for ourselves. The more comfortable we are with our own values, the easier it is to allow others to live by theirs.

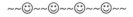

Attracting Happiness

Here's a story my friend Rob told me that illustrates the power of being the thing we value. Rob was telling me about a friend of his who is a monastic—someone who has chosen to live in a religious community, apart from mainstream society, living a life of faith, study, and service to others. His vocation calls him to bring his beliefs to the world in a way that makes a positive difference.

He explains, "When I talk about what I believe and why I do what I do, people become uncomfortable and they turn away. But when I live my beliefs and model those in my behavior toward others, people are attracted to me." In other words, because what he says and what he does are aligned, people are drawn to his energy and genuineness.

I have seen that phenomenon occur in my own life and business. For many years, I focused on telling, selling, and teaching. Frequently, I encountered others resisting "my message." I had to learn to let go of needing to be *The Expert*. Now, I focus on BEING happy, on BEING a good listener, on BEING a coach and educator, and, with far less effort, I am more successful than ever. I more clearly spot good opportunities, and the right opportunities seem to spot me.

I passionately wish that same good feeling for you, my dear reader, in your life!

Great Places To Work

"To me, the most important thing is consistency between your belief system and your behavior. You can develop all kinds of lists of core values. But ultimately, the most important core value is a genuineness to deliver on what you say your core values are. Being genuine builds credibility and trust."

~~Buddy Pilgrim, CEO of Simmons Foods Inc.

 Based on my 25-years' experience of corporate and consulting, I classify organizations into three categories when it comes to values:

A. Those with great written values but leaders who behave in ways that contradict what's written down—there's a huge gap between enacted and espoused values.

B. Those with written values that are modeled by the top leaders, but poorly communicated to everyone else—which shows up as a disconnect between behavior at the top of the organization versus action on the front lines.

C. Those with values that are modeled by leaders, talked about frequently, woven into all training and decision-making, and owned by the entire employee population—these are *great places* to work.

Which description best fits your organization? How are your values brought to life?

Here's an example of a company that fits the last category. Ritz Carlton Hotels (decades ago) created systems that weave the organization's values into everyday life and bring them alive. At every pre-shift meeting, every day, five minutes are spent reviewing one of the organization's clearly defined values. Over the course of a year, with no formal training, a typical full-time associate will have spent over 20 hours immersed in understanding and living the Ritz Carlton Credo.

Try This: The Ritz Carlton Approach: Whether you are a small business owner, a front-line associate, a top leader, or a middle manager, you can try the following in your own part of the world. At every meeting (daily huddle, morning minute, weekly staff, project/committee, etc.) for the next 90 days, take five minutes to review your organization's vision or mission statement, or one of its core values.

You might simply review the value, or have someone tell a story about the value in action. Ask someone to reflect on how they might live that value in the next week, or have everyone write down one action, large or small, they'll take today to support it. Be creative—take just five minutes today and in 90 days, you will have spent five hours focused on bringing the organization's values to life in your part of the world. Notice how the very fabric of your organization changes. To take a look at the Ritz Carlton Credo, go to: http://corporate.ritzcarlton.com/en/About/GoldStandards.htm

So remember...

ANYONE CAN BE A LEADER WHO LIVES EVERY DAY THE VALUES THEY ESPOUSE

~~☺~~☺~~☺~~☺~~

Despair.com

OK, you might be thinking, "Why plug a site called *despair.com* in a book that's supposed to help me learn to be more Happy." But you know, good (clean) satire has an important place in our world.

If you've ever seen the Successories™ line of framed prints—breathtakingly gorgeous photos paired with inspirational quotes—then you must visit this site, where similar photos are paired with very *different* quotes. Take your sense of humor with you and remember that three seconds of laughter is equal to three minutes of aerobic exercise! http://www.despair.com/indem.html

~~☺~~☺~~☺~~☺~~

Happiness ③ Principle

Live For Life Not Stuff

Americans are exposed to nearly 5,000 marketing images everyday on TV, on billboards, in newspapers, at sporting events, online – even when we pump gas into our cars! What is the main message most of these ads are sending? You are incomplete… You are missing out… You are inadequate… unless you buy/use/wear/eat our product.

Really? If I don't have a home espresso maker or a 72″ plasma HDTV am I really incomplete or less adequate than someone who does? What's up with this?

I have news: You and I are NOT inadequate. You and I are just fine, as we are. Every study ever conducted on the subject of motivation comes to the same conclusion—for most of us, money does NOT buy happiness. Oh, it can help us feel good in the short term, and some money is necessary for the basics of life; but if you are not happy with WHO you are, more stuff won't help you be happier. So, how does one Live for Life? Here are some tips:

Create a Joy List. Make a list of all the things that bring you Joy. Review it and add to it regularly. Notice any patterns that emerge (and notice how few of the items on your Joy List involve 'stuff' versus people or experiences). Then focus on creating more opportunities for yourself to engage in what nourishes you. And keep adding to the list over time.

Note: I know some people who have grown their list to 150+ items and who read it every day as part of their daily ritual.

Focus on Internal versus External. "Keeping up with the Joneses" is a lifestyle that leads in only one direction—down the path to "never quite there, never enough." Instead, base what you want on what is important to YOU.

Challenge Yourself to Notice What You Have. Ask: "In what ways is my life perfect, as it is, right now?" You may surprise yourself with how long your list gets!

Memories Trump Souvenirs

A few years ago, I spent a holiday in Ireland with my eldest daughter, Kelly. She had just completed a year of study-abroad at Trinity College in Dublin. We spent a week together touring the southern and western coasts of the island, and stayed at Bed & Breakfasts in whatever town we were passing through at suppertime. We got lost several times, but each time we made a discovery that we would never have if we had stayed on our planned path. We created some wonderful memories together.

During our adventures we did a bit of shopping. Various Celtic gifts were bought on Grafton Street's famed pedestrian mall in the heart of Dublin; hand-crafted crystal picked up in Waterford; Irish wool sweaters at the Blarney Woolen Mills; and Royal Tara China direct from the source in Galway. These were all beautiful things, and for a guy rose in an Irish family it was incredibly exciting to purchase this stuff in the Old Country!

But as I reflected on what I took away from the trip, it wasn't the purchased goods I treasured but the memory of how Kelly and I accidentally (not on purpose!) drove past the Waterford Crystal works and went in on a whim.

The gifts purchased in Dublin, however, paled in comparison to the fun we had touring the Guinness factory at St James Gate, and encouraging Kelly as she forced herself to drink her first real pint ("I CAN'T leave Ireland without drinking a Guinness, Dad!"). And the sweaters were nice, but the fun part was that they were made from the very sheep we kept meeting on the road.

What are some of the memories you've created? Look to those as another source of oxygen for yourself!

~~☺~~☺~~☺~~☺~~

Penny For Your Thoughts

Leaders recognize that money doesn't really make people happy. It provides short-term pleasure, but not long-term motivation. For the past decade, average annual merit increases have been fairly flat. Handing out 2% raises does not get people excited.

Try This: When it's your turn to deliver the news, don't apologize. Instead, be curious. Find out what people really want. Maybe it is more time off for travel, or to work on a really cool project, or to cross train with another team or department. Maybe it's working a more flexible schedule, or attending a personal development seminar. Then build those motivators in to your culture, and address them at the next performance review.

From the June 23, 2003 *Fortune Magazine (Ask Annie)*: "Don't depend on external rewards. You'll never have enough control over them, because luck, market conditions, and executive decision-making above you will always play a role. So find something you can be proud to do whether you're highly rewarded or not. It's a lifelong process."

So remember

LEADERSHIP IS NOT ABOUT A TITLE... ANYONE CAN BE A LEADER WHO HELPS OTHERS TAP INTO THEIR OWN MOTIVATION!

~~☺~~☺~~☺~~☺~~

Go Here, View This: http://www.youtube.com/watch?v=tkzr0naZnZ0

What you will see is one of the coolest Rube Goldberg machines ever created, clearly built by people who value *precision*. It's an award-winning Honda commercial from a few years back. There are no computer graphics or digital tricks in the film. Everything you see happened in real time exactly as you see it, in two-minutes. It required 606 takes to have it all work perfectly. Tip: turn up the sound when you watch it.

~~☺~~☺~~☺~~☺~~

—Chapter 3—

Identify And Eliminate The Frictions In Your Life

Principle #4.   Be Early

Principle #5.   Build Reserves

Principle #6.   Tolerate Nothing

Friction is a Physics term defined as, "A force that resists the relative motion of an object." Friction gets in the way of movement. It drains away the energy of an object in motion; increasing friction ultimately stops all forward motion.

The following principles address the reduction of friction; in other words, things you can do to eliminate wasted energy and free it up so you can redirect it to creating happiness!

When you are late, behind, under the gun, or overwhelmed you are using a lot of energy just to keep up. Being Early is about recapturing some of that lost energy for yourself.

Worry is another big drain. You'll learn that having Reserves for your physical, mental, and emotional hot buttons can prevent a lot of friction from occurring.

Finally, when you are moving fast, it is easy to lose track of little annoyances and then get used to living with them. Little issues become big issues, and then you defer addressing big issues because you don't have the time. Pretty soon the accumulation of little things equals an enormous drain on your energy—the friction can bring you to a halt. Tolerate Nothing will teach you how to reduce your friction load through awareness.

When you implement these three principles you will find you have more energy to keep moving at the Speed of Life.

~~☺~~☺~~☺~~☺~~

Happiness **4** Principle

Be Early

This principle is not (just) about arriving early for scheduled events. It is about adopting a mind set and behaviors that eliminate what I call "delay friction" or "lateness stress."

What do I mean by those terms? Let me answer your question with another question. What is something in your work or life that you are putting off? Starting a project? Finishing it? Training in a new software or workflow process? Having a difficult conversation? Making a career change?

Step back and take a look at what you are carrying around with you as a result of that delay. Some of the stress may be from the project or situation, of course. But be honest with yourself: how much stress comes simply from the fact that you are putting it off? I know that for me, the stress associated with an overdue project or delayed conversation is often far, far greater than the stress associated with actually doing the thing!

So… what if you raise your hand to go first (or maybe second) on the rollout schedule, instead of 12th? What if you schedule that conversation for tomorrow morning instead of spending part of every day worrying about it? What if, instead of digging in your heels and resisting that new process, you simply surrender to it and channel your resistance energy into implementation? The results could amaze even you, eh?

And the best part is, when we let go of delay anxiety, we open more space for happiness. Early speakers are more likely to be graded by objective standards. As more people give their presentations, there is, naturally a bit of comparison in the grading (oh, that was good, but Suzy's was a bit better!) Plus, once their presentation is over, early presenters can sit back, relax, and learn a bit from other's presentations. Those who go last, meanwhile, sometimes learn less. While the others are presenting first, late presenters are nervously going over their notes, rehearsing in their heads, and creating negative self-talk ("Oh, those are really nice charts … mine aren't that good. Wow, Suzy's is so good; I'm so not ready). Their anxiety builds and builds as they wait their turns.

I can't say how many times one of my kids came home and said, "I am so glad I went first!" Gradually, each of them came to champion the benefits of being early. They learned to put their energy into meeting their goals rather than procrastinating on them.

You don't have to be first all the time, but it is important to know it is an option. When you have a chance to be first but you hold back, you open up a space that is too easily filled with regret, worry, anxiety, and concern. The lessons we instilled in our children can benefit everyone who is caught in the fear of public speaking or anything else they are reluctant to do.

Do This For Yourself

Volunteer to be first. For whatever it is. The benefits to you are many:

Save Wasted Time And Anguish—no nail-biting worry while you wait for your turn.

Occasion To Shine—when you are early, there is nothing in front of you that you/others would compare.

Quick Relief—you can relax and bask in the relief of completion as you watch (and learn from) those who follow.

You're The Expert—confident, enthusiastic early adopters are often perceived as experts as much for their courage as for their content.

~~☺~~☺~~☺~~☺~~

Preparing For The Unexpected

A client recently brought to our coaching conversation a load of anxiety about upcoming workplace changes. The key problem for him is not "how to handle change"—rather, the issue is that his company is a "player" in the mergers and acquisitions (M&A) world, and what can happen in six months is both unknown and, in this moment, unknowable. Further, M&A activity is handled at the top level of the organization and is shrouded in secrecy. My client, a senior leader one level below the executive committee, shared, "I can't prepare my division for what is coming when I don't know much myself. And for what little I do know, I am sworn to secrecy since no paperwork is signed and nothing is certain. The staff knows 'something is going on' and morale suffers."

Turns out that the "story" he tells himself is that he can't take action until the news breaks, then everything will have to happen at the last minute. His nightmare implementation scenario was the source of his stress. "Well," I asked, "what CAN you do while you are waiting? How might you prepare for the unknown?" Once he dropped his "can'ts" and started thinking in terms of getting ahead of the changes, he realized that he could proactively get his team ready for the next set of changes.

He created a plan to engage his "inner circle" of managers in an examination of various M&A outcomes, then pulled out the issues common to all, and started to prepare the staff. Some education in change management benefited everyone, regardless of what specific changes actually occurred. And he also decided to focus on team building to strengthen the team in advance of upcoming challenges.

Here was an example of *being early*. Change is inevitable, so when you prepare for "change"—even in a general way—by giving people tools, language, and processes for better handling the unexpected, you eliminate a stressor and create space for a bit of fun. And even, dare I say, happiness?

~~☺~~☺~~☺~~☺~~

Evolution Of Fame On The Internet

 Most people are familiar with YouTube.com, the online video repository that allows anyone in the world to experience their 15 seconds of fame through self-posted video? Have you seen the *Wunderkind* of posted videos, the six-minute "Evolution of Dance" routine? A comedian named Judson Laipply posted his routine online, and ended up on *Good Morning America* and on the cover of *Rolling Stone*. His is a classic story of the power of the Internet to create fame. Many imitators came after, but he was first—he was early to the online video "game."

If you love popular music, you should see this one. You can find it linked from about a million places on the internet, but the prime source is Laipply's original site, www.theevolutionofdance.com. And turn up the volume on this one—it is a blast!

Happiness **5** Principle

Build Reserves

"Keep a green tree in your heart and perhaps a singing bird will come."
~~Chinese Proverb

What do you worry about? Many people live their lives a step away from feeling overwhelmed or going over the edge.

- Are you living from paycheck to paycheck?
- Do you feel exhausted all the time because you barely fit in six hours of sleep each night?
- Does your significant relationship get only what you have "left over" after you put in a full day at work?
- Are you a business owner who doesn't do marketing because "there's not enough time?"

These all show up as worrying… about money, relationships, health, the future, whatever. Worrying is practically a national pastime. It drains energy and often creates barriers to feeling happy. I don't believe there is a cure for worrying, but there is something you can do to reduce the impact (and perhaps even the frequency) of worry in your life: Build Reserves.

What is a Reserve? It is defined as: *something set aside for the future or for a special purpose,* or *something retained for oneself.* Reserves can be physical, mental, or emotional. You create a reserve anytime you invest ahead in yourself, which creates future capacity.

How does one create reserves? Try these tips:

Pay yourself first. No matter how much or little you earn, you *can* afford to set aside something for your future from every paycheck. Participation in a company retirement plan is a must—why pass up the company match? Have just five or ten dollars from your paycheck deposited into a Christmas Club account, and you'll have $250 to $500 show up just when you need it at year-end.

Plan re-fueling time. Set up a standing date with your spouse/partner once or twice a month. Use that time to connect, communicate, and invest in the relationship. That way, when daily or bigger issues arise, you'll be able to work through them more easily and from a place of greater trust.

Go on a monthly date with your child(ren).** Just as with your partner, but your focus should be on creating memories through the special times you create together. Have a few old standbys, zoos, museums, and parks, but also pick new places where you can all experience new sights and smells—pick-your-own-fruit farms, a new museum, or simply bake cookies together.

When you build Reserves into a relationship you create a foundation for future times when there may be periods with less contact or when you violate a promise. That reserve will help keep the relationship strong.

**If you're not a parent, create memories with nieces and nephews, the children of your friends or a neighbor who affectionately call you Aunt or Uncle, with grandchildren, and with Little Sisters or Brothers.

Stock slightly more than you need. Identify what you most worry about running out of—cat food, candles, toilet paper, toothpaste, panty hose, pasta, or peanut butter—and stockpile those few items. Buy a little extra when it's on sale or buy in bulk. Always having enough on hand takes the edge off your worry. Every line of worry that you can shut down opens capacity for you to be happier and less stressed.

~~☺~~☺~~☺~~☺~~

Creating The Space For "Happy"

Of the thirteen happiness principles, I personally find this one to be the most difficult. It is hard enough to keep up with the present, let alone creating capacity for the future! Yet when I am successful at building my own reserves, it is often the most rewarding of the principles. Because of past medical problems, I worry constantly about my health. When I feel tired or physically off-balance, my runaway imagination can immediately turn that fatigue or ache into major medical problems (yikes!), which saps my energy and my creativity.

I've learned over the years that I need to create reserves to ensure I feel well and don't lose a lot of time obsessing over whether or not that pain in my ankles is arthritis, or the two-day headache is a brain tumor (I told you my imagination can run fast!). For that reason, I work hard to make sure I get a minimum of seven hours of sleep each night and I work out three times a week. Anything less, and I feel it physically and mentally. Plus, I know that when I work out—even when I "don't have the time"—that I will have more energy, a better attitude, and will feel less stressed. What I do today is about how I will feel two days from now.

My wife, Cheryl, worries most about the kids. When they were younger and all living with us, it was not so bad, since she saw them safely into bed each night. But then they each started off to college, and suddenly there was no more daily physical contact. As you can imagine, there were many sleepless nights. "Why haven't I heard from them? What might have happened?" These were the worried questions that nagged at her. How did we create a reserve to reduce her worry? We got our own toll-free number! Now there were no excuses for not calling home and it was more cost effective than long-distance calls back and forth (today, of course, they all have mobile phones!)

And now, with all three kids out of the house and living in different cities, we have set up regular touch-points, and the kids tell Cheryl their schedules for the upcoming week. As long as Mom knows what's happening and check-ins occur as scheduled, she has the capacity to NOT worry in-between. And we all know the first rule of families, right? *If Mom's happy, everybody's happy!*

~~☺~~☺~~☺~~☺~~

Balancing Your Relationship Checkbook

 Without people, you can accomplish little. But when you figure out how to truly connect to your team, well… the sky's the limit. Relationships are key to that connection, so it is important for leaders to build solid rapport with their team. Starting a new workplace relationship is like opening a bank account. When a new employee starts, they are actively recruited, warmly welcomed, and paid attention to, which results in an initial balance of 1,000 "points" in their account with you. Every time you do something positive—recognize effort, give useful feedback, provide encouragement, offer a sincere compliment, give credit where due— you make a deposit into that employee's account. When you make a mistake— assign blame, criticize unfairly, take credit yourself, fail to obtain resources—or have to deliver bad news, you make a withdrawal. If the balance dips too low, your account gets "closed" with that person. You may not know when it happens, but from that point forward they are disconnected from you and the organization. Ouch!

Try This: Use the end of the year (or the start of the new year) to make a big deposit in the accounts of your team members. I call this "annual re-recruitment," and here's how it works:

Visit every person on your team. Shake their hand warmly, look them square in the eye, and say, "I am so glad you are here. You are an important part of my team, and I appreciate you and your efforts. I look forward to working with you for another great year!" Are you perfect? No. Might you make mistakes this year? Probably. Will people forgive you your mistakes? If you've got enough on deposit with them, they will most certainly work through the rough times with you.

So remember...

LEADERSHIP IS NOT ABOUT A TITLE...	ANYONE CAN BE A LEADER WHO SPENDS SERIOUS TIME BUILDING POSITIVE RELATIONSHIPS

~~☺~~☺~~☺~~☺~~

Creating a Good "Front Porch"

Scott Ginsberg wears a name tag. Go here if you'd like to say hello: www.hellomynameisscott.com. Scott wears one every day. You know, the "Hello My Name Is..." stick-on type that most people don't like to wear? For Scott, it started as an undergraduate classroom in the Fall of 2000, and his experience was so rich that that he now wears that name tag all the time (A true Millennial, he even had it tattooed on his chest for when he goes swimming!). After multi-thousands of days of wearing a name tag, Scott has parlayed his experience into a full-time speaking career, and he's authored several books on approachability and is a featured contributor to *Cosmo* and *Fast Company* on, you guessed it, approachability.

Scott's experience reminds me of the ten years I spent wearing a different button every day back in the late 80s and early 90s. It gets people talking with you. Check out his website to learn what a good "Front Porch" means, and whether you have one!

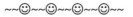

~~☺~~☺~~☺~~☺~~

Happiness 6 Principle

Tolerate Nothing

Tolerations are the things we put up with in our lives that create friction, thus slowing us down, impeding our forward progress. Frequently, it's the stuff in our lives that exists just under the radar—stuff that annoys us yet, is not pressing or important enough to take care of. Some examples: the piles of papers on the desk, the dirty backseat in the car, the unresolved disagreement with a coworker, the project that sits one step away from completion.

 A while back, during a conversation with my coach, I caught myself whining (yes, I do have my whiny moments!) about feeling stuck and about lacking motivation. He suggested I needed to "do Tolerations." Brilliant! I thought, yes, that's exactly what I needed to do—unclutter my brain and open up some creative space. I dug into the tolerations exercise and began noticing a feeling of lightness in my work as I applied what I knew to my situation. In *The 13 Principles of Happiness*, number six states:

Tolerate Nothing. Continually identify and eliminate all the little "stuff" which causes you friction and drains your energy.

One of the items on my list of tolerations was that a living-room rearrangement had put my favorite space very near the television, rendering it essentially useless as a quiet spot for reading or writing. More on my situation later, for now a bit more about tolerations…

Tolerations are typically small things individually that, when added together, create major friction in your life. Imagine your life as a computer running many programs at the same time. Each program is using just a few mega-fragments of energy and memory, but open enough of them and keep them running, and suddenly your 'computer 'slows or even freezes. Most people are, at any point in time, carrying around dozens—perhaps more than a hundred—tolerations. That's a lot of open programs creating friction in the brain!

How do tolerations affect us? Maybe you've heard the story of the boiled frog? The story goes that a frog will remain in a pot of water as the water temperature is slowly raised to boiling. The cold-blooded frog's body temperature adjusts as the heat is increased and he doesn't even realize he's in danger. We, too, grow accustomed to our environment even though it may not be a good idea to remain. We can be blind to seeing the clutter in our brains, relationships, physical space, commitments, and so on.

What are you tolerating? If you removed a few tolerations, how much better would you feel? Think about it. One less burden to carry on your shoulders; more space, energy, and capacity to focus on what is really important; more space to feel happiness and contentment rather than the anxiety and stuckness that often accompanies tolerations. And who doesn't want to be happier?

~~☺~~☺~~☺~~☺~~

The Tolerations Exercise

Take a piece of paper and write at the top,

"What am I tolerating in my work or life that I am no longer willing to tolerate?"

Avoid editing yourself, just write. Carry the list around with you for at least a day. Visit all the different "environments" in which you live—office, car, home, work and personal relationships, financial, fun… and notice what you are "putting up with" in each area. Write down everything you notice – large, small, and in-between (Important note: this is NOT a "to-do" list; it is an awareness tool. So don't worry about How, right now… just list the What).

Review the list for any themes that emerge. You might prioritize by noticing which items bother you the most. Ask yourself, "What do I want to do about <this> and by when?" Consider your four options: Do, Delegate, Defer, or Dump:

Do: Take action to remove the toleration—have the awkward conversation, change the unhealthy or unproductive behavior, remove the clutter, clean it, replace it, buy it, or whatever is required to remove it from your list.

Hint: You'll find that many tolerations will sort of "take care of themselves" once you've identified them as such, even if you do not put them on a task list. In fact, if you put the list away for 30 days, I promise that when you pull it out you'll find several items from the list have disappeared. That's because tolerations remain so because we've simply become used to them, and once they are back in conscious awareness, we naturally take action to "scratch the itch." You'll find that eliminating tolerations is incredibly energizing!

Delegate: Turn over the item to someone else to take the action on it. Delegate a household task to a child, partner, or contractor. Automate it (like setting up all your utilities, car, house, insurance payments to automatically come out of your checking account) or create a system to complete the action.

Example: My father-in-law realized that he hated mowing the lawn and shoveling his walk in winter, so he hired a landscaper to mow and plow, and then sold his lawn mower at the next family garage sale!

Defer: When you do not have the time, resources, or energy to address the toleration today, you can put it off for a while. Pull out your calendar/planner and set a timeline to perform a future action to eliminate the toleration. Then forget about it until it pops back onto the radar screen.

Note: This is not about continuing to "put up" with it—it is about *choosing* to intentionally defer action until a more appropriate time, e.g., saying, "I don't currently have capacity to handle this. I'm putting it on my list for November. Until then, it will not bother me because I know I will take care of it then."

Dump: Finally, you may find that once you've assembled your entire list that some individual items simply pale next to the entire collection. You might look at some and ask, "In the grand scheme of things, does this really matter to me?" When your response is "not anymore!" then you can give yourself permission to no longer consider the issue a toleration. Cross it off. Done. Let it go.

Ok, back to my living-room arrangement. So what did I do about my toleration? I shared my concern with my wife, Cheryl, and after a short conversation we decided our set of stereo headphones would be a practical tool to address my issue. Some nights she plugs into the TV while I read, other nights I plug into the stereo for music to mask the sound of the TV. And of course, some nights we sit together with a dish of fruit and cheese and take in a movie together! Toleration done. I only have 70+ others to address. I can feel more positive energy flowing already!

~~☺~~☺~~☺~~☺~~

A Tolerating Culture

Tolerations spread quickly in the workplace. What starts as a simple issue can escalate into full-blown trench warfare and a long-term toxic work environment. So it is important to address tolerations when you become aware of them.

One of my clients worked for a small company of fifteen employees. The office space they occupied had one shared washroom. Two employees were known to continually leave the washroom in a less-than-ideal condition. It might not seem like much, but in fact their actions were disrespectful and inconsiderate to the other employees. Yet everyone tolerated the "delicate situation." Finally, my client got fed up and confronted the employees. The behavior changed and morale in the office improved.

Consider this behavioral experiment. Five monkeys are put in a cage. Bananas are placed at the top of a platform. When one monkey attempts to climb to the platform, the other monkeys are sprayed with water. When another monkey tries for the banana, same result. Eventually, any time a monkey tries to get to the platform, the others attack. One by one the original five monkeys are replaced. None of the original monkeys that had been sprayed with water remain. The new occupants, who have no knowledge of the spraying, continue to attack anyone who attempts to get to the bananas.

I remind people that this story is a fable of how corporate culture is created and maintained. It also begs the question, are you doing things in your workplace just because "that's the way they've always been done"? Well, you can break the cycle. Encourage your coworkers to challenge and eliminate workplace tolerations. If you do, I'm sure you'll find your work environment a much more pleasant and productive place to be.

So remember...

LEADERSHIP IS NOT ABOUT A TITLE... ANYONE CAN BE A LEADER WHO BUILDS A RESPECTFUL WORKPLACE CULTURE

~~☺~~☺~~☺~~☺~~

Entertainment For The Curious Mind

Do you know what happens when you mix Mentos™ candy with Diet Coke™? The result is... well, I'll let you find out. (If you're reading this in the midst of a cubicle village, keep the volume down on your speakers—the musical accompaniment is hard to ignore). http://www.eepybird.com/dcm1.html. The main video is Experiment 137. If you enjoy this experiment, you might also want to check out The Domino Effect video on the same page. Do these guys look happy, or what?!

~~☺~~☺~~☺~~☺~~

–Chapter 4–

Notice and Use Your Power to Choose

Principle #7. Choose to Respond

Principle #8. Stimulate Your Development

Principle #9. Pay Attention

Principle #10. Simplify

Do you recall the scene from "The Wizard of Oz" (1939) where Dorothy is seemingly stranded in Emerald City after the Wizard in the hot air balloon takes off without her? Glinda, the Good Witch of the North, explains to Dorothy that the ruby slippers she's been wearing can solve her dilemma. Glinda tells her, "My dear, you've had the power all along."

Like Dorothy, you have access to great power—the power to modify your response to events, to change your environment, to shift your attention, and to focus in new and different ways.

Once you understand your power and how to access it (and no, clicking your heels three times won't get you there!), you will never be a Victim again. Instead, you'll own the power to move from emotional reaction to rational response.

These next four principles will help you learn to intentionally leverage the power that you already possess, yet rarely access—your own "ruby slippers."

Happiness 7 Principle

Choose To Respond

"The problem is not that there are problems. The problem is expecting otherwise and thinking that having problems is a problem."

~~Theodore Rubin

Anyone who has been to a comedy club or seen an episode of *Who's Line Is It Anyway?* on TV has witnessed improvisational acting. In the theatre of Improvisation, the basis of nearly everything is a technique known as "Yes, and…" For the actors making up a skit in the moment, the goal is to *keep the drama going*. The players must embrace whatever comes at them and figure out how to incorporate it into their next line or action. Life is no different—as it speeds ever onward, we must keep the drama going; the tone, the mood, and the outcome of that drama are the direct result of how we respond.

The opening line of one of my favorite books captures the essence of this perfectly:

> *"Consider this, if you will: You are on stage every day performing the scenes of your life in a play without a script."*[3]

What a concept, eh? What if you could *consciously* tap in to your natural ability to create, and focus it on making every response a positive one? Try it for a week, or even just a day, in the drama of your life. Rather than reacting to the scenes as they unfold, try embracing what happens and keep the scene moving.

When you practice responding long enough, then response becomes the reaction. The difference between reacting and responding is often little more than a pause to take a deep breath and to *think*. In that moment, during that pause, the trick is to shift from Telling ("You have to do this next") or emoting ("Ohmigod! You did WHAT?!") to Asking ("Can we talk about this?")

What Does "Choosing To Respond" Look Like?

Come From A Place of Curiosity—Formulate a question, so that what others see is your curiosity and support. "What have you already tried? Can you tell me what happened? How can I support you? What are you looking for next? What are the issues on the table that we need to review? What is the outcome we are seeking here?" You get the picture? As this habit becomes more natural, you can *respond* even under the most urgent of circumstances.

Example: While watching an episode of *ER*, I was paying attention to how incoming patients were treated on the show. If the patient was conscious, the doctors poured out a constant stream of questions so that, even as they were reacting with textbook precision to the symptoms presented, they were increasing their understanding. Thus, each successive action became more a response to the true needs of the situation and less a blind reaction to what was on the surface.

Redefine Your Self-Talk—When your usual reaction is "NOW what?!" replace that with "Now HERE is something interesting!" Replace "Woe is me!" with "What are my options?" Instead of, "Why is this happening to me?" try, "What might I do with this situation?"

Embrace That You Are Human—When you miss a day of exercise or succumb to the lure of something your diet forbids, remember that success is not about quotas. Notice that you are making generally good health decisions, and let go of the guilt that might discourage your continued progress.

Try a Non-Habitual Response—When a friend or spouse doesn't live up to your expectations (my wife says this never happens to me ;), notice your reaction. Do you blurt out something like "You ALWAYS <do this>" or "You NEVER <do that>"? What's a different way to respond? Try asking questions rather than making assumptions.

Improving Relationships

Anyone who thinks surviving the "terrible twos" is the biggest challenge in parenting hasn't lived with a teenager! As a parent who steered four kids through their teens, I speak from much experience when I say that choosing to respond can make a significant difference in your relationship with your son or daughter. When my youngest son said, "Dad, the <...> is the fastest car!" I would say, "You should never drive fast." When he would say, "All my friends can...." I said, "I don't care what other kids do, you can't." My reactions usually ended conversations but not the conflicts.

I had to work very hard to learn to stop reacting to what I didn't like and to respond to my son in an inquisitive and non-judgmental manner. When I did, the results were amazing. Now, when he said, "Dad the <...> is the fastest car!" I asked, "Oh really? How fast does it go?" When he said, "All my friends can..." I asked "Which ones? And, "How long have they been able to?"

These responses seem simple yet they had a significant impact—they encouraged conversation. By *responding* to my son instead of *reacting* to what he said, we began to better understand each other and our relationship became stronger.

~~☺~~☺~~☺~~☺~~

Look Forward Hopefully

Earlier in my career I managed an outplacement center for my employer. Over the course of 18 months I worked with more than 500 people to help them create resumes, search for new jobs, and move on with their lives. After a while, I learned I could predict who would "land" a new position more quickly based on the conversations we had following their termination. If their tone was, "I was screwed!" and they sold off all their company stock in anger, they hung around the outplacement center for a long time. When their first question was, "Can you help me understand my options?" I knew they would soon be healed—and hired. This latter group *chose* to move forward rather than react.

An Idea-Friendly Workplace

Ideas are fragile. Like seedlings, they need warmth, light, and nurturing to grow. If you step on a seedling, you crush it. An idea stomped on too early will die, even if the idea was a good one.

Nurture Ideas Using "Yes, And..." Try this at your next team meeting: When a new idea is tossed out, nurture it before you analyze it. The rules are that you must say "Yes (embrace it), and…" then put on what Edward de Bono calls the Yellow Hat of Optimism. Then, for two to four minutes, you must focus on the following questions: "What is GOOD about this idea? Why WILL it work? What are the benefits of doing it? How might this idea be improved to make it better?" After those first several minutes, notice how much stronger the idea is. Okay, now you can put on your Black Hat of Assessment and critique it.[4] A weak idea may still die, but notice how many seedlings do grow to maturity or produce stronger offshoots because you chose to respond with a nurturing *Yes, And*, which allowed them to grow stronger.

So remember...

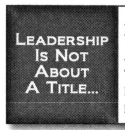

LEADERSHIP IS NOT ABOUT A TITLE...	ANYONE CAN BE A LEADER WHO KEEPS THE CONVERSATION ABOUT CHANGE IN FRONT OF THEIR TEAM EVERY DAY, SO THAT BIG CHANGE HAPPENS IN SMALL PIECES OVER TIME

~~☺~~☺~~☺~~☺~~

Happiness **8** Principle

Stimulate Your Development

Stimulating your development is not just about taking a class or attending a workshop, although both are very useful tools. Rather, it is about examining all the environments in which you operate and questioning which ones are feeling incomplete or stuck for you. Once you have identified the areas where you are feeling stuck or stagnant, you can then take action to pull yourself to a different level. It's about challenging yourself to evolve and to adapt to new environments, new people, and new ideas. Pay attention to what happens as new paths and opportunities reveal themselves; these will allow you to grow and develop in new areas. To best serve yourself, you sometimes need to *provoke* yourself to evolve.

Here's something I've been doing to be a better global citizen—I'm reducing my carbon footprint by hypermiling. If you haven't heard about this, let me explain briefly. Instead of rushing, braking, fuming, and accelerating as I drive from appointment to appointment, now I go slower, avoid braking, and coast in neutral to avoid stopping, unless necessary.

Now, I'm an extravert and I'm a "busy guy," so I was used to moving fast, then getting frustrated when others ahead of me were not moving as fast. I have relearned how to drive my car so that I conserve fuel by using hypermiling driving techniques. I have shifted my thinking about how I can get where I need to be on time and conserve fuel.

Hypermiling maximizes fuel efficiency. Instead of pedal-to-the-metal and brake hard, I've been using techniques such as pulse & glide, coasting in neutral, slowed acceleration, and timing my arrival at intersections with traffic lights. It requires me to pay more attention to the road, as I must adapt what I'm doing to my driving environment. This is not driving on autopilot — I am more conscious and aware of what is going on around me. Am I driving uphill or downhill? If I'm approaching a traffic light, will it still be green when I arrive, or will it likely be red? Am I going fast enough to avoid irritating the drivers behind me? I also find myself keeping more distance from the cars in front of me, as I seek to avoid braking except when necessary.

This technique has not impacted my travel times. I still arrive as planned, because much of the time I used to spend idling at red lights I now spend slowly coasting to the light in neutral. Instead of my usual style *gofast. stopquick.wait*, which involved a lot of rushing, braking, fuming, and then accelerating, I'm now doing more *go, glide, go.*

As I drive more mindfully, I am extremely aware how different that feels. Funny thing—as I pay closer attention to my driving and the environment on the road, I find myself paying closer attention in other areas of my life, like conversation. And as much as I consider myself as a good conversationalist, I know that greater improvement is possible.

~~☺~~☺~~☺~~☺~~

Ideas to Stimulate Your Environment

Put Yourself Into Situations That Spark Your Creativity. Drive a different route to work. At work, eat lunch with a different group of people than usual. Watch a program on PBS instead of a network "reality show." Shop at a different grocery store. Ooh, here's an interesting one. When you visit the same food store every week, you eventually are able to shop with half your brain because you know where everything is. It becomes easy. When you try a different store, let go of the irritation you feel because things "aren't in the order you're used to." Instead,

41

notice all the different products that are not available at your usual grocery. Notice how things are organized: better? The same? Worse? What possibilities might this exercise open up for you?

Surround Yourself With People Who Continually Challenge and Energize You. Being happy is something you have to choose. You can work hard at making that choice everyday, and succeed—but if it's always about you, all by yourself, that can get tiring. People provide you with emotional support. Seek out and spend time with people who are happy themselves, and who are exciting to be with. You know who they are—the ones who laugh easily and smile often. On the flip side, if you notice that a friend or colleague seems to slow you down or drains your energy, figure out what is going on and make the necessary changes.

Write Visions, not Goals. Years ago, all motor vehicles were driven from the rear wheels—power was transferred from the engine (in front) through the transmission to the rear axle, allowing the rear wheels to *push* the vehicle forward. Today's vehicles are predominantly front-wheel drive. By concentrating the engine's power into the front axle, vehicle control and flexibility are improved, passenger space inside the car has opened up (no more sitting on the hump!), and fuel consumption decreased. It is just more efficient to be *pulled* forward than to be pushed from behind.

Our lives work the same way. If we are constantly focused on tasks and steps and endless to-do lists, then it's all about the work, which is exhausting. Money, success, winning, meeting deadlines, and losing weight are examples of goals that push you forward. But when we focus on our vision, the thing that rouses our passion, we are literally pulled forward. Joy, happiness, fulfillment, good health, and community are examples of affirmative goals that pull you forward.

Create A "Happy Place" For Yourself. We all need to retreat from the world every once in awhile. For some of us that may be taking a walk in the fresh air; for others it's a phone call to a friend, journal writing, dreaming of a vacation spot, remembering the story behind a family photo, reading a new novel, or taking a long drive while singing out loud a favorite song on the radio over and over again. Whatever yours may be, set up a happy place you can easily access, physically or mentally, when you need to reenergize your attitude. All you need to do is go to that place, and let the energy of that activity or environment do the work to shift your mood.

Distinction: Provocation Versus Overwhelm

 I walked into my family room one day to send a fax. My son, Jared, was slouched in a chair (as only a teenager can slouch) in front of his computer. Hip-hop music blared from the speakers, while on the other side of the room a movie played on the TV at high volume. Jared was playing an online video game with a buddy. He was also conducting several Instant Messenger conversations on the side. AND he was on the phone with someone. He was doing all this and still tried to carry on a brief (yet unproductive) conversation with me! This story is NOT an example of the principle, but I relate it to make that distinction clear. Jared was *over stimulated*, and he was not moving forward. The idea here is not to add stuff to the point of overwhelm, but rather to keep reinventing and renewing your sources of happiness and creativity.

An Invitation To Provocation. The word *provoke* means "to excite; to call out; or to stir to action." And in many ways, that is what this principle suggests. Poke yourself, provoke yourself, stir the thick stew of your life to bring new things up to the surface. Look for new opportunities that pull you outside of your usual routines or old perspectives. Invite yourself to experience something new and give yourself permission to change as a result of that experience.

Avoid complacency. Keep creating a more intriguing future that pulls you forward. What defines happiness for you today is different from what it may be tomorrow, so keep playing and experimenting. Be open to the reality that you are aware of only a small part of what life has to offer. If you always stay where you are, you may be missing the opportunity to try on new paradigms and life experiences, which might better match where you are going rather than where you have been.

Another way to look at it is through a phrase I've used in training programs for many years to help motivate participants to adopt a new behavior or two. The last slide of my presentation reads in large letters:

IYADWYADYAGWYAG!

Curious? See if you can finish the statement: "If you always do what you've always done…" That's right!… you'll always get what you've always got!" So, when there is any aspect of your life that you find stagnant or difficult, or which brings you unhappiness, then stop and think: "How might I approach this differently?" Thanks for playing!

~~☺~~☺~~☺~~☺~~

Innovate Or Die!

"Stuck thinking" is the deadliest of all organizational diseases, and one of the most common. We constantly walk a line between consistency and predictability (some of which is necessary for organizations to function) versus innovation and change (necessary for organizations to grow). How might you increase your impact if you could stimulate fun and innovation?

43

A Workplace Exercise: Next time you are in a problem-solving meeting and the discussion feels like a summer re-run (been there, done that!) try a Random Connection exercise. Here's how it works in four easy steps:

1. First, agree to leave the problem alone for a few minutes.
2. Next, ask someone to name, say, a random animal, food, electronic appliance, or tourist destination.
3. Spend the next few minutes at a white board or flip chart examining the randomly chosen topic thoroughly.
4. Return to the old issue and use the diversion to make new connections.

For example, someone picks "dog." What are some characteristics of a dog? How do dogs behave? What do dogs do for fun? Where do dogs go? Who do dogs hang out with? …You get the idea—have some FUN with it for a few minutes.

When you run out of ways to examine your random topic, return to the original problem and ask: "In what ways might we apply these <dog> ideas to our work issue?" or "How might a dog address our challenge?" Put people to work on making connections, and notice how "unstuck" they become.

You don't have to wait for a group meeting to try this. Stuck while sitting at your desk? Open a dictionary to a random page and select the first noun you see. Spend 3–5 minutes brainstorming its characteristics. Then return to your problem and notice how many new ideas come up, now that you have stimulated all those synapses in your brain!

Put yourself in the place of a coach, and ask: "How might I stimulate others' creativity? You might:

- Bring a bag of kids' toys to your next staff meeting and let everyone play with something during the meeting.
- Invite a guest speaker from another department to open some understanding of how you all connect.
- Take your team on a field trip to another company, and look for ideas that are different from what you are doing.
- Send a team to a mall or amusement park for the day and ask that they each return with 10 new ideas on Customer Relationship Management.

So remember...

 **LEADERSHIP IS NOT ABOUT A TITLE...** ANYONE CAN BE A LEADER WHO KNOWS HOW TO SLOW DOWN, PAY ATTENTION TO OTHERS, AND DO EVERYTHING THEY CAN TO INCREASE THE EFFECTIVENESS OF CONVERSATION!

~~☺~~☺~~☺~~☺~~

Happiness  Principle

Pay Attention

How did you get to work today? Did you drive? What do you remember about your drive to work? Was there anything different or unusual? How many school buses did you see? Were there any new billboards along your route? What building along your way has the most interesting architecture? If you are like most people, you are probably thinking, I don't know, I just drive; I don't pay attention to that stuff.

 Paying attention means turning off the autopilot to see more fully what is around you. My family has spent nearly 30 years vacationing in coastal North Carolina. We love to go crabbing. It's a lot like fishing — you sit on a pier then drop your line into the water with a chicken neck or thigh tied to it (crabs are scavengers so they don't mind if their chicken is a bit less than fresh). Wait a bit and then pull in the line. If there is a crab hanging on to the chicken, you net it and put it in your bucket, then repeat the process until you have enough crabs for dinner.

Crabbing can take from a couple hours to several, and sitting out on the pier, watching the water and scenery can be quite peaceful. But this story isn't really about crabbing, it's about turning off the autopilot to see and appreciate what is going on around you that you may not have noticed before.

On a recent trip, we were out on the pier as the tide went out. That's usually the time we pack up and leave as the crabs go underground or out with the tide. This time, we stayed on the pier and were amazed at how the peaceful scenery of the saltwater marsh we had enjoyed for so many seasons exploded into an abundance of wildlife. The muddy flat that emerged from under the water was teeming with life! Birds of all types quickly moved in to hunt for any morsels left behind. The quiet rustling of the marsh grass was replaced by a myriad of bird noises. What we had always considered as a smelly dead zone was really something quite beautiful when we took the time to notice.

Three Blessings Exercise

This is a quick exercise for people who want to strengthen their awareness of good in the world. It's also recommended for those who constantly live on their dark side; and it is a powerful exercise for teenagers. I've used it with one of my own children and my wife. The Three Blessings exercise conditions the positive-emotion muscle and is simple to do.

Instructions: Every day for 30 days[1], sometime near the end of the day, write down three good things that happened for you that day; just three good things. They can be huge, like, "My sister delivered a healthy baby after a very difficult pregnancy." Or they can be really simple, like, "I saved a little money for my future today because my boss paid for my coffee at the coffee shop this morning."

Three Blessings...

- Every day for 30 days
- Three things that went well
- Trains your positive emotion muscles
- Increases awareness of what IS
- Expands capacity to notice more, and focus less on negative

Even little things can be important. "Somebody said 'thank you' to me today and it's the first time that person has ever done that." Got it? Do it every day for thirty days. You don't have to do anything else with it—the writing it down is the exercise.

What happens if you do this for thirty days? At the end of the exercise you will notice that you are more aware of the positive things in your life than you were before you started. You may also notice that you're starting to actively look for—and enjoy—those little positives *as they occur*, thus experiencing more moments of happiness throughout your day. Hint: Accumulate items from your Gratitude list to create the Joy List mentioned in Principle 3—your permanent collection of things you enjoy.

~~☺~~☺~~☺~~☺~~

Here are some additional practices that might help you pay more attention and notice the beauty around you when you turn off the autopilot:

- *Meditate for a few minutes*—witness your breath, your body, your mood, your thoughts (not evaluate, just observe).

- *Be a tourist in your own life for one day*—pick up a camera and document your day in pictures, noticing (as if for the first time) all the interesting stuff you do and the people and places you often overlook.

---

1 You don't even have to do it every day; research shows that if you write in a Gratitude journal even just four-five days a week, it still works wonders toward strengthening your Positive Emotion muscles..

- *Visit your workplace as a reporter/journalist* (with an objective perspective) for one day.

- *Notice when your mood is up or down* and ask: What was behind this? Is this how I want to feel? (NOTE: you are not responsible for the emotion you are in, since emotions just happen to us automatically. You ARE, however, responsible for noticing it and moving out of it or choosing to stay with it because it serves you).

If you are on autopilot, you're no longer paying attention. Everything just happens. It is only when you pause and look—really look—that you can experience awe and wonder and beauty in your life... and create the opportunity to shift your perspective.

~~☺~~☺~~☺~~☺~~

Pay Attention On The Job

Three Blessings is also a great exercise for a leader's toolbox. Give it to someone who is at-risk or doesn't work and play well with others. Task them to do this for 30 days and when they are done ask them to tell you if their job is as bad as they thought. They're going to find good things, and may be a better employee for it!

The Leadership Version: Before you initiate negative action with a member of your team, take time to capture three things they do well, or three things they contribute to the team. The issue at hand must be addressed, of course, but when you take the time to remind yourself of why you first hired this person and what they contribute, the conversation you have will be built on a more positive, supportive foundation.

So remember...

| LEADERSHIP IS NOT ABOUT A TITLE... | ANYONE CAN BE A LEADER WHO LOOKS FOR THE GOOD IN OTHERS. |

~~☺~~☺~~☺~~☺~~

Rainbow Sunsets

 On a plane trip home from a coaching conference, I witnessed a most spectacular rainbow sunset. From my seat on the west-facing side of the plane, I had a panoramic view of the horizon. The sky was edged at the upper cloud line in a deep indigo, below which ran a wide swath of dark crystalline sky blue. There followed successive thin stripes of brilliant green, sun yellow, bright orange and then, right at the horizon, a rich, deep red. This rainbow stretched across the horizon, to the right and left, as far as I could see. The view was breathtaking.

In that moment, I felt well up inside of me an enormous sense of gratitude for the beauty that is in the world. The feeling was so intense that I was moved to tears. Sitting alone on a plane 20,000 feet above somewhere, I cried for joy that I have the gift of sight. It was that extraordinary.

~~☺~~☺~~☺~~☺~~

Happiness 10 Principle

Simplify

"Too much … too, too much!" Do you ever find yourself thinking that? Who we are is a result of choices we make and the way we surround ourselves with stuff and challenges. Sometimes our choices can leave us busy and full, yet unhappy. That's when we need to start dropping what does not serve us.

Think about the things that complicate your life—tasks, goals, relationships, commitments, and expectations. How many of those feel like appendages on the rocket, splaying out in all directions to catch the atmospheric resistance, increasing friction, and slowing you down?

To simplify is not necessarily to give up goals, material possessions, or busy schedules, and move to a *yurt* in the desert someplace. Rather it is a reminder to keep what we have and what we do in perspective. Simplify is about striving to remove the clutter in our lives in order to concentrate our energies toward those things that really matter.

In Karen Kingston's book, *Clear Your Clutter with Feng Shui*, she explains, "All that 'stuff' you're hanging onto is draining you! Get rid of it. Simplify and declutter, and expect things in your life to change for the better."

Tips To Help You Simplify

Tips & Tools

Schedule "Nothing" Time. Establish time in your calendar to do nothing. Learn how to be at ease in solitude, silence, and stillness. Realize you don't need all that "noise" around you to feel content.

Let Go of Goals. We typically get 80% of the impact from 20% of our goals. Line up your personal goals and identify the handful that will provide you the most return on your time investment. Cross off the rest. A narrower focus will increase your output and creativity while reducing your stress.

Create Space. In *Clear Your Clutter with Feng Shui*, author Karen Kingston walks through a non-judgmental review of all the places in life where 'stuff' accumulates and then provides a template to help clear it out. Feng Shui is, according to Kingston, "the art of balancing and harmonizing the flow of natural energies in our surroundings to create beneficial effects in our lives." Clutter is what "accumulates when energy stagnates and, likewise, energy stagnates when clutter accumulates." Clutter, then, can be a symptom or a cause of Stuck Energy.[5] And stuck energy holds us back from truly enjoying life—it gets in the way of happiness. When we live a simple life, we increase our opportunity for awe.

Outsource What Doesn't Serve You. What business is Me, Inc (that's you) in? While you might know *how* to pay bills, clean house, and mow the lawn, consider if these tasks bring you joy. If no, why not automate or delegate them? Have your monthly bills automatically debited through the bank, delegate vacuuming to someone else or hire a cleaning service to come in once a month, and pay the neighbor's kid (or a lawn service) to cut your grass. Spend one hour and forty bucks to have a professional tax service handle your returns this year, and then spend the 20 hours you just freed up to do something that DOES bring you joy!

~~☺~~☺~~☺~~☺~~

Nature Abhors A Vacuum

 I've employed the principle Simplify for many years to help pull myself out of creative funks or to open up opportunity. Whenever I cleared something out—reduced, moved, delegated, eliminated, or finished—the most interesting things have happened.

Feeling overwhelmed at work? I look around the office for signals, and usually notice all the junk that's built up over several months, like piles of filing, projects not stored away, unread reading piles, and an army of Post-it® notes stuck to everything. All that stuff, subconsciously, distracts me. If I take a few hours on the weekend to clear it all out (usually several trash cans full) I find that my workspace transforms, and everything flows better.

No new business coming in? Once, when I was in a dry spell, I dug into my "prospective client" files, just as marketing manuals instruct. I was on my third or fourth unproductive call when the alarm bells sounded in my head, "I'm hating this. These people did not connect with me then, they aren't going to now." As I began filing the folders, I noticed that my client files were crammed in like sardines. So I took a deep breath, and before I could evaluate my own action, I purged all the inactive leads and "maybe someday" items, and dropped them into a storage box.

Gone, off my list, let them go. As I reveled in the new-found space, I noticed something odd. My phone suddenly began ringing. Within a week, I'd filled my calendar, and ended up having my busiest quarter ever. In conversation with a colleague, I wondered about the connection between clearing out my files and the sudden surge in business. She told me it was because, "Nature abhors a vacuum." As long as I held on to those old leads, my (mental and physical) space was full. But once I created an empty spot, the universe noticed, and natural forces conspired to fill that space.

I've also applied Simplify to my clothes. I've had items in my closet that pre-date my eldest child, who's long graduated from college. You probably have some of these, too: the favorite old sweaters, the comfortable shoes that look like hell but fit like…. Well, anyway, I purged out everything I haven't worn in two years or that I've been "saving for when...." My closets and drawers are now lean and mean, and the time it takes me to put away or pick out my clothes has dropped to half. I simplified, yet gained in the process. I wish the same for you!

~~☺~~☺~~☺~~☺~~

How Many Balls Can You Juggle?

Ah, you expect so much—of yourself and others—on the job. How much of the stress you experience comes from trying to juggle too many roles, goals, and projects simultaneously? Take a hard look at your current goals. Remind yourself that your maximum capacity is four to six priorities at a time. Identify the top four and renegotiate the rest with your manager or affected clients. Then focus your energy on those four. When one is completed, pull another off the list, and never hold more than four at a time. You will find that you get more done (and at a higher quality) by working on ONLY four priorities at a time than you did when you tried to juggle ten or twelve.

Why is this true? Let's go back to physics: when you eliminate the friction (i.e., resistance, discontinuity, resource, and schedule conflicts), between those multiple, simultaneous priorities, the energy that used to go into unproductive juggling now goes into *doing*.

Here's an exercise you can do at work. Choose an associate who appears overwhelmed. Put yourself in the place of a coach, and ask: "What would you be able to accomplish tomorrow if you only had to worry about ONE THING?" Draw out an answer, then help them structure the next day around that single focus and protect them from distractions. This may not be a drill you can do often; yet you will be amazed at the payback from your efforts

So remember...

LEADERSHIP IS NOT ABOUT A TITLE...	ANYONE CAN BE A LEADER IF THEY MODEL EFFECTIVE HABITS AND SHARE THEIR GREAT IDEAS WITH OTHERS

~~☺~~☺~~☺~~☺~~

Thou Shalt Not Whine

A couple of years ago the Reverend Will Bowen, a minister at the One Community Spiritual Center in Kansas City, Missouri, vowed to model the sort of behavior he encouraged in others: he made a pledge to go 21 days without complaining. That meant no whining, gossiping or criticizing for three weeks, long enough to form a new habit.

"The one thing we can agree on," said Rev. Bowen, "is there's too much complaining." It took him three-and-a-half months (!) to string together 21 consecutive days with no whining.

Other members of the church decided to join him, and they commissioned purple bracelets (they read, "A Complaint Free World") to wear as reminders. A local paper did a feature on the group's initiative, which was eventually picked up by *People Magazine*, and then *The Today Show* called. Suddenly this little church community was besieged by requests for bracelets, and they set up an entire website to supply the world. They've now sent several million bracelets to people and organizations all over the world.

Check out: http://acomplaintfreeworld.org/ where you can order bracelets or learn how to use them. Basically, you wear it as a reminder. Catch yourself complaining or kvetching? Switch to the other arm and restart your count. Keep switching until you reach 21-consecutive days. Simple, though not easy.

This campaign, in my humble opinion, is a form of Simplifying. When we eliminate complaining, we free up that energy for ourselves to enjoy what's right about life. And that's another path to Happiness!

~~☺~~☺~~☺~~☺~~

—Chapter 5—

Be, Boldly, The Real You

Principle #11. Speak the Truth

Principle #12. Focus on Today

Principle #13. Be Authentic

If you have done the work to get to this place, that means you've fueled your oxygen tank, eliminated some of the friction(s) in your life, and taken ownership of your power to choose how you show up in the world.

You are stronger, carrying less baggage, and you feel more in control. The final three principles will challenge you to build on what you've done so far and now show up fully as who you really are – unafraid, and willing to show the world the Real You rather than the masks or roles you feel you're "supposed" to wear.

If you live these last three principles, you will notice that you are:
• More "comfortable in your own skin"
• Clearer in your priorities
• Ready to let go of the future needing to be a certain way
• More present to enjoy what IS to the fullest
• No longer afraid
• No longer comparing yourself to others, and thus…
• Far more comfortable respecting others' values
• You are happier!

Happiness **11** Principle

Speak The Truth

Premise: You can be totally honest and unconditionally constructive at the same time.

First, a distinction: *Telling* the truth is about being honest when you communicate. *Speaking* the truth goes a level deeper. It compels you to actually say what you are thinking, even if what you have to say is unpopular or will be met with resistance. How often do you have regrets because you did not speak up, or didn't say what you really wanted to say? Have you ever found yourself in a difficult situation because you had earlier avoided saying what needed to be said? Part of happiness is accepting where you are at any point in time. It is about telling *yourself* the truth, as well.

Who Decides What Is Truth?

Several years ago there was a media controversy surrounding the Mel Gibson-produced movie, *The Passion of the Christ*. Depending on what you read, watched, or listened to, the movie was: a religious experience or an example of bloody cinematography run amok; worthy of five stars or only two; an historically accurate retelling or a flawed and biased account; a work of great vision or merely a vehicle for profiteering from the related merchandise sales. It is difficult not to feel the pull of multiple truths around us.

What is the truth? We felt great confusion in America when the US-led coalition invaded Iraq (justified war or violation of international law?); we feel conflicted when a loved one dies after a long illness (a tragedy or a blessing?); and our self-talk comes from two directions when we institute our own transitions, e.g., when we left our last job to start a new business (bold move or insanity?).

Which is THE truth? Fact is, multiple truths can, and always have, existed together. It is possible to hold a thing to be true for you *and* simultaneously understand and acknowledge other people's truths. Religion, politics, marriage, entertainment—all are examples of institutions where people believe in their own truth, yet recognize that others have their own version that holds validity.

Speak the Truth does not mean you must personally lay claim to the "one-and-only" truth. It simply means that you will be happier if you acknowledge what you see to be the truth *for you*, and be comfortable saying it to others.

Caveat: if your "truth" is harmful to others, then maybe you should go back to Principle #2, Live Your Values, and examine what is truly in your heart. The reality is that you will experience more peace and contentment when you speak up and behave in ways that honor your own values versus what others have imposed on you.

~~☺~~☺~~☺~~☺~~

How Does One Speak The Truth?

Just Do It. My mother always used to quote Mark Twain to me: "If you always tell the truth, you never have to remember anything."

Vote Your Conscience. Do or don't do something based on *your* truth, not somebody else's.

Say What You Know Others Feel. Especially when you know that others agree with you, yet no one is saying anything, call up the courage to break the silence. No problem is solved unless it can be named.

Stop Playing Games. Begin by facing the truth about something you are doing. Ask yourself, "What's really behind why I am doing <this>?" When you get to the root issue, you'll be able to address it more effectively than if you keep lying to yourself.

Look Beyond Your Fear. Try to focus less on the embarrassment you might feel if people react to what you say. Instead, remind yourself that if no one speaks up, nothing will improve. Look past your fear to what the situation will be like once you've addressed the issue. You'll be happy you did.

~~☺~~☺~~☺~~☺~~

My Truth Forms My Reality

A few years ago I joined a Mastermind group of entrepreneurs. We met weekly to help each other grow our businesses. We would focus our collective creative energy (aka "the Mastermind") on the issues, problems, or opportunities of one member at a time. In addition to addressing our respective business challenges, we decided to do a group study of the book, *The One Minute Millionaire*. This book challenged me to examine my own myths and beliefs about money.

My *truth* is, I was raised poor and Catholic. I was taught that wealth is something that only vain and selfish people acquired. My *truth* is, I'm embarrassed to speak of financial success. My *truth* is, I've always feared that if I acquired wealth, I'd become, "one of those selfish rich people."

Well, as long as I held those beliefs, I'd behave in ways that pushed wealth away. Why would I want to be rich if I think rich people are undeserving, right? The *truth* was, for me to change my behavior, first I had to change my thinking. I looked away from the Leona Helmsleys and Paris Hiltons of the world (people who showcase selfish material wealth) and looked instead to the Rockefellers and Carnegies (who gave away most of their wealth) and the new holders of wealth such as Warren Buffett and Bill Gates who pledge their billions to make the world a better place. I made a written commitment to become an Enlightened Millionaire (one who shares rather than hoards). My truth about wealth shifted from, "I'm not that sort of person," to, "Imagine how many people I could help!"

I now know that facing the truth about my own thinking has allowed me to take the first step: giving myself permission to think BIG!

A question for you: *In what ways might you be denying yourself something important in life simply because you haven't told yourself that it's okay?* **
**e.g. to fall in love ** to take on a big project ** to be a leader ** to go on a cruise ** to return to school ** to lose weight ** to be happy.

To learn more about Mastermind Groups, see Christine Zust's article at http://www.emergingleader.com/article21.shtml for an overview.

~~☺~~☺~~☺~~☺~~

Say The Words, "I Can't"

 I once managed an operations team during a period of near-supersonic growth. I was putting in obscenely long hours and was constantly under water. In the dictionary, the word "stress" had my picture next to it. To top it off, I felt very isolated.

At one point, we all met to review a major technology project. As we went through all the work that was to be done for the rollout, everyone busily took notes and nodded their heads. "Sure. No problem. I can do that." Everyone sounded so confident and competent.

"It's just me," I thought. "I'm such a loser!" I could literally feel the air being sucked out of the room. Then my accounting manager spoke up: "I'm already so deep in backlog that it will be months before I come up for air. There's simply no way I can manage this!"

What happened next was like a dam burst. The room filled with cries of agreement and wails of despair. I grabbed a marker and we started capturing issues on a flip chart. Two hours later we emerged from the meeting laughing and happier. Did we solve our backlog problems? Not entirely, though some new plans were made. What I learned from the experience was that most of our stress came not from the backlog of work, but from the feeling that each of us believed we were alone in our struggle. It was the proverbial "elephant in the room"—everyone knew it was there, yet as long as we did not say it out loud, we could avoid having to deal with it. Once someone Spoke the Truth, that elephant lost its power to intimidate.

Try This—What is an important issue plaguing your workplace that no one wants to talk about? How might you bring that issue to light? Be bold, be brave, and be the one to say, "Houston, we have a problem!" Then watch that elephant shrink right before your eyes.

~~☺~~☺~~☺~~☺~~

Happiness 12 Principle

Focus On Today

"The best things in life are nearest: Breath in your nostrils, light in your eyes, flowers at your feet, duties at your hand, the path of right just before you. Then do not grasp at the stars, but do life's plain, common work as it comes, certain that daily duties and daily bread are the sweetest things in life."
~~*Robert Louis Stevenson*

How do you complete this sentence:

"I know I will be happy when __<fill in the blank>__." Write it down if you'd like, we'll come back to this later.

What is the best use of your time now? I mean right now? Today? Well, clearly in addition to reading a great book on choosing to live a happy life, the best use of your time now is to refocus on what's most important. Important for yourself and important for others. When we get caught up in the tumult of deadlines, office politics, family dynamics, personal crises and the latest disturbing news, we can lose sight of what is important for us.

Let's start with today. What's on your plate? Responding to your emails? Making some client calls? Picking up your children after school? Finishing the next chapter in the latest best seller? Praying? Stopping by the grocery store for an emergency supply of tofu and hummus? OK, so that last one is what's on my plate, but the idea is that what is important to each of us crosses all dimensions of our lives—our professional obligations, our family responsibilities, our creative interests, our spiritual commitments, our community involvements, and our personal aspirations.

Happiness in life begins with your happiness today. You might find it difficult to focus on your happiness today, however, if you're distracted by the stress of multiple demands. The simple task of taking a deep breath, spending a few minutes to think about today, and listing what is most important for you to complete before the end of the day can help sustain your creative enthusiasm.

How might you focus on *your* happiness right now, today? Here are some ideas.

Tips & Tools

Plan Daily Happiness Checks. Check in with yourself throughout the day to assess your happiness and, if you're feeling particularly low, take a moment to re-energize.

Notice And Shift Your Self-Talk By Just One Degree. If you catch yourself thinking, "I'll be happy when..." try shifting that to "I'll be *happier* when...." It is great to look forward to a better future, yet what power there is in acknowledging that you are already happy, right now!

Savor The Moment. When you notice yourself feeling good or enjoying an experience—no matter how small that experience is—try slowing down for just a minute. Bask in that moment*. Give yourself permission to enjoy it, with all your senses, before moving on. This is how we create memories.

*For example: admire the beauty of deep red rose; breathe deeply the special smell of fresh-mown grass on a summer day; listen to a chorus of birds as they greet the morning; enjoy the smiles and laughter children playing a game; examine the face of your grandmother as she shares a story of 'the old days; or feel the special glow your body carries right after a brisk walk or a good workout.

Remember: Everyone gets the same 24 hours every day. How we choose to use that time—especially to increase happiness for others and ourselves—will determine our satisfaction with our lives. No better time to start changing our world than today. Let's do it, together.

Happiness Was There All Along

My favorite children's book of all time is Maurice Sendak's wonderful *Where the Wild Things Are.* I've read it so many times that I've memorized the entire work. My eldest daughter wrote a beautiful essay about the book as part of her college application, so the book continues to be a part of my family's life even as my children grow into adulthood. Sendak's hero, Max, was upset with his mom because she would not let him get away with mischief. When sent to his room, he used his powerful imagination to leave his mom behind and to go to a place where he could play all the time.

Max might have been telling himself, "I'll be happy when I get to call the shots!" Yet, even after he got what he thought he wanted, he found happiness eluded him. So he left the Land of the Wild Things and returned home. There he discovered that happiness was, in the end, as simple as a warm supper and the security of family. The moral of this story is this: Happiness is often right under our noses; but we must choose to pay attention to it!

So, back to the beginning of this section: how did you answer the question I posed? How did you fill in the blank? I know I'll be happy when: I get that promotion? Lose weight? Get a raise? Land a new job? Meet my soul mate? Have kids? Finish this project?

I have news for you: waiting for something to happen tomorrow so you can be happy is like watching yourself in the mirror and saying, "You go first."

Happiness is not a place. It's not a destination. It's not a goal or event. Happiness *is.* It is a way of *being.* It is a mode of traveling. If, instead of focusing on "when" or "if," you focus on today, right here, right now, you know what? You can be as happy right now as you decide to be. You don't have to wait.

If I don't do anything else today, acknowledging that my wife and I built a home together, where four of the most beautiful people I will ever know felt safe enough to share a meal, our lives, a story, and knowing that this, my friends, this is the most important thing for me, for today, forever ... well, then I've had a happy day. How about you?

~~☺~~☺~~☺~~☺~~

Making Room For Happiness @ Work

"If you only look forward to tomorrow, you'll collect an awful lot of empty yesterdays."
~~Professor Harold Hill in "The Music Man" (1962)

I have many friends in the accounting field, and my wife is a CPA. All of these people are immersed in the tax season and year-end close from mid January until mid Spring. During this incredibly intense work period, I've witnessed two different approaches to the peak demands of their season:

Group A: Works long hours and weekends; heads down; intense, relentless pressure; no time to breathe; feeling burned-out; dragging themselves to work, and always, always, always looking forward to April 15th when the pressure will ease up. Then, on April 15th a huge collective sigh goes up and these players collapse into a heap.

Group B: Works long hours and weekends; heads down; intense pressure; bi-weekly pizza parties; the occasional Silly Hat day; random acts of fun; and a looking forward to April 15th when the pressure will ease up. Then on April 15th a huge collective sigh goes up, and the teams looks around to determine what their next challenge will be.

Same pressures, same tasks, totally different outcomes. What's the difference? Group A companies think that during times of intense pressure, fun and enjoyment wastes productive time and must be banned from the workplace in order to "get real work accomplished." They believe that happiness must wait until the job is done. Meanwhile, Group B companies realize that, during times of intense pressure, fun and enjoyment help keep creative energy at higher levels. They recognize that happiness can be connected to progress as well as outcome.

Think about what your team is currently under pressure to complete—it may be a reorganization, implementing a new process, a high-profile project with a no-compromise deadline, or getting through a seasonal peak of business. While there is a temptation to delay all "celebration" until the goal is reached, consider how you might recognize achievement of milestones along the way, or how you can toss a little bit of Play into the Work environment.

Taking a moment to have fun and be happy without having to wait till the end can do much to "refill" everyone's current energy reserves such that they can avoid burnout and complete the job at higher levels of quality and productivity. Bottom line: Happy people do better work.

For more on Play at Work, see the tips list at http://www. creativityatwork.com/articlesContent/playwork.htm

So remember...

LEADERSHIP IS NOT ABOUT A TITLE... ANYONE CAN BE A LEADER WHO INSPIRES HOPE AND OPTIMISM IN OTHERS (AND THEMSELVES!), EVEN IN DIFFICULT TIMES

~~☺~~☺~~☺~~☺~~

Happiness **13** Principle

Be Authentic

Authentic: adj. ~not imaginary, false, or imitation; genuine, bona fide; being actually and precisely what is claimed.

What does it mean to be authentic, to really "show up" as yourself? And what does that have to do with Happiness?

Well, consider that many of us spend parts of our lives playing different roles. For example, we might show up as the caring service rep for a client, as the wise counselor for a friend, as the concerned parent, or even as the dutiful child. We typically do so because the part we are playing is one that we took on voluntarily—we sought the Service Rep job because we like to serve; we want the friend to succeed; we chose to parent the child, and so on.

When we play a part of our own writing, it can be a source of joy. What happens, though, when we find ourselves pretending to a role that does not fit us? Think about a time when you felt stuck with a project/task that you did not believe in, or working with an individual or team whose values actually violated your own. How did it feel? If you are like most people, you felt drained, even exhausted by the experience of having to pretend. You may have found yourself constantly on edge, carefully guarding your words and how you reacted to others to avoid friction. It probably required enormous amounts of energy to play such a role.

The energy tied up in playing uncomfortable roles is energy that is not available to us for moving forward. Plus, if we play the role for too long, we can get confused about what part is really us and what part is the role.

Be True To Yourself!

"To thine own self be true, and it must follow, as the night the day, thou canst not then be false to any man."
~~William Shakespeare in *Hamlet*

Tips & Tools

Some questions to help you examine your own authenticity:
- Have I been doing something that goes against my values?
- What roles do I play that do not match who I am?
- Whom do I know that I can trust to ask if they've seen a change in me recently?
- What message(s) from myself have I been ignoring?
- What action(s) might I take that would increase my comfort level?

~~☺~~☺~~☺~~☺~~

Happiness Was There All Along

I worked with a client who loved the company she worked for. She received a promotion that required a move to a new division. Within a few weeks she realized the culture of teamwork and service that had so engaged her in her old job was completely missing in the new division. Here, team meant, "shut up and do what the boss says." She came to our conversation and said, "Working here is like buying a car from one of those dealerships where they tell you how to fill out the Customer Satisfaction Survey." The subtle message was, "You better give us all 5s—or else!"

So every day, she pretended to be a happy camper just to keep her job, saying, "Yes" to the division head even while her stomach churned over the disrespectful behavior her fellow managers dished out.

Then one day she showed up to our conversation in a panic. "I yelled at one of my staff today. Actually yelled! I am so upset—this is not me, but I feel like I'm falling into the same behaviors as everyone around me."

Within the safety of our coaching conversation she was able to disconnect from her reaction and create a strategy to stop her "slide into the black hole." She went back and spoke privately to several of her peers whom she suspected were also unhappy. Armed with the certainty that she was not alone, she had a conversation with the division head to share her concerns about how her (the leader's) style was affecting her own and others' behavior.

It was an intensely uncomfortable conversation. However, the division head thanked her for the feedback and asked for ideas on how to change the situation. The boss did not change overnight, but she agreed to open up discussion and listen to others' opinions and ideas before putting out a decision. My client reported that her energy levels at meetings went way up, as she now felt like a she could contribute rather than expend all her energy keeping her mouth shut.

So remember...

LEADERSHIP IS NOT ABOUT A TITLE...	WHEN YOU HONOR THE REAL YOU IN YOUR THOUGHTS, IN YOUR ACTIONS AND IN YOUR RELATIONSHIPS, AT HOME, AT WORK AND EVERYWHERE, YOU REINFORCE YOUR FOUNDATION FOR EXPERIENCING AUTHENTIC HAPPINESS

~~☺~~☺~~☺~~☺~~

Technology Improving Lives

 A couple of years ago, former Microsoft chairman Bill Gates delivered an address at the Tech Museum of Innovation in San Jose, where he received that museum's James C. Morgan Global Humanitarian Award for his philanthropic work through the Bill & Melinda Gates foundation.

Gates' speech was reprinted in Fortune Magazine. As I read the article I felt inspired by the work Bill Gates and his foundation are doing, and also awed by the immensity of the issues—his billions are but a drop in the bucket of what is needed for some parts of the world. I was most impressed with the degree to which he seems to care about the state of the world, and especially children. Sure, he has the resources to help more than most people, but the fact is that most people don't even bother with the issues he and his wife have taken on. He seeks to help with funding as well as by leveraging his celebrity status to draw attention to horrendous situations that can often be addressed with very simple technology and allocation of resources.

Gates appears to be a leader who cares. Bravo!
http://money.cnn.com/2007/01/09/magazines/fortune/Gates_philanthropy.fortune/

—Chapter 6—

Happiness-Building Skills, Exercises And Practices

In the Introduction, I spoke of the parallel between our physical body and our emotional self. Both require that we exercise them regularly if we want them healthy, balanced, and strong. In this chapter you'll find a sampling of exercises[6] that will, if practiced regularly, increase your experience of Happiness and other positive emotions.

For quick reference, here are the one-dozen practices contained in the chapter:

1. Listen To Your Emotions

2. Let Go To Create Space For Happiness

3. Appreciate All Emotions, In Balance

4. Pay Attention to What You Take In: Detox, Oprah, And The Search For Chocolate

5. Do a Teardown and Rebuild of Your Life: Nine Lessons From a House

6. Practice Thanksgetting: The Skill Of Accepting Gratitude

7. Give More Than "Just Enough"

8. Smile: Happiness Is Not A Spectator Sport

9. Give and Receive HUGs: Human Understanding Given

10. Stop Trying So Hard: Evolve Into Happiness

11. Take Your Oxygen Daily

12. Practice The Skill Of Savoring

Practice #1—Listen To Your Emotions

"In the last decade or so, science has discovered a tremendous amount about the role emotions play in our lives. Researchers have found that even more than IQ, your emotional awareness and abilities to handle feelings will determine your success and happiness in all walks of life."
~~John Gottman, Ph.D.

Excerpted from a discussion at a client's office: "Emotions don't play a role in our decision-making, Jim. We make decisions here in a very straightforward manner, based on logic and reason and an objective review of the facts. Actually, I'm a little *frustrated* that people keep bringing up emotion, as I don't see that as relevant to our process. I'm much *happier* when we deal with our reality instead of some touchy-feely fantasy world."

Do you see what I see? The only way this manager could fully express his perspective on emotion was to invoke emotion—he's frustrated; he's happy. But hey, he's never emotional....

The fact is that we are emotional beings, just as much as we are physical and intellectual beings. We are always in some emotional state. Our emotions are an integral part of us—they serve us, protect us, guide us, inspire us. Emotions set the stage for much that happens in our own little world.

Our word *emotion* comes from a Latin word meaning, "to move out from" or more casually, "that which moves us." An emotion is a predisposition for action—every emotion carries a different story, a different language, and a different set of options for action.

The same event can lead to a wide variety of responses because each person involved is predisposed to interpret the event differently based on their emotional lens. For example, the announcement that Jane, a peer, just got a promotion.

~Chris, who lives often in anxiety, gets all wrapped up in worrying about how he's going to handle the additional work that will be dumped on the team.

~Liz, whose primary mood is enthusiasm, can't wait to go over and congratulate Jane, even though she also holds some bitterness as she feels she was equally qualified for the promotion.

~Shaniqua is carrying a streak of jealousy today, and secretly begins to plot how to make Jane pay for leaving the team.

~Jon, who has worked closely with Jane and really respects her ability, feels a sudden surge of sadness, and sits frozen because he doesn't know what to do with that feeling.

None of them are paying any attention for the rest of the meeting.

Throughout this book, I use the term *positive emotions* to describe the emotions that cluster around Happiness, such as gratitude, enthusiasm, optimism, hope, contentment, joy, etc. But that term implies there is an assessment or valuation of the emotion—some emotions are good and some are not. The reality is that emotions are neither good nor bad; emotions are just emotions. There they are. Each one serves a purpose. It's better to withhold assessment of an emotion and to ask:

"What message is this emotion sending me? And how might that be impacting me?"

In the example above, Jon's sadness is telling him that he is in touch with something he has lost. And that he may need to give himself space to grieve for that loss before he moves on. Meanwhile, Chris' anxiety is telling him that he is afraid, but not sure exactly where that's coming from. So he may need to initiate discussion about how Jane's duties will be distributed so he can deal with facts instead of fears.

When we pay attention to what our emotions are telling us, we expand the information available to us in our actions and decision-making.

Applying the Skill: Keep an emotions journal—document your emotions following any event, conversation, etc. Note the emotions you feel, and what actions you took, or wanted to take from that emotional space. What happens when you acted on it? What happens when you did not? Are there emotions you don't want to act on?

Practice #2—Letting Go To Create Space For Happiness

I donate blood regularly and am often rewarded with a free t-shirt. Because I donate blood regularly, it created a problem for me, a small problem but a real one: my t-shirt drawer was crammed full. I removed two older shirts and decided to recycle those as workout shirts. Another problem: the shelf I keep my workout gear on is crammed full.

While in my closet, I noticed the three new dress shirts I recently purchased are freshly pressed and are hung on the closet handle with a note from my wife: "Can't fit in closet. Something has to go!" I know what this means. I don't want to admit it, though. You see, each item in my closet has a story. "It used to be my favorite shirt," or "I bought that on our cruise," or "it still fits!" or "my mom gave that to me..." If I continue to honor every story for every pair of pants or socks or t-shirt, I'll have no room for any new stuff. So I must let go.

When it comes to clothing, I follow the rule, "if it doesn't make me feel fabulous, it should go." Well, what if I love it all? Sorry, Jim—you either create some space or you are stuck with your current wardrobe for the rest of your life; or we cram it in and you'll always be wrinkled. I must let go. Aargh!

65

I can purge other areas of my life, but clothes I wear till they die. I still own a pair of jeans I bought before I had kids, and my eldest is in her late twenties! Maybe it's my upbringing (large family, hand-me-downs were the norm), maybe it's a comfort issue, I don't know. I do know this, however: If I don't let go of *something*, there's no space for anything new. So, I will let go. Next time the Salvation Army calls about used clothing, I'll say, "Yes, please."

What does this have to do with happiness? Here's the thing: no one who lacks for happiness has an empty emotional closet. Typically, your closet is full of the emotional 'stuff' you've brought home over years and decades, and there's simply no room for happiness. Do any of these stories match what's hanging in your emotional closet? "It used to be my favorite emotion" or "I bought that when I was in high school" or "It still fits!" or "My Mother gave that to me..." Get my drift? You are always wearing some emotion, but if you limit yourself to what's already in your closet and you can't bring yourself to let something go, you'll never have the space for the new emotions you want to bring home!

~~☺~~☺~~☺~~☺~~

Letting Go, Clean Out Your Emotional Closet!

Go through your emotional closet and pull out the items that no longer make you feel fabulous.

Let Go Of Certainty—If you find yourself paralyzed by analysis, please know that you will rarely know everything, and there will always be some risk in life.
Replace with: "I know that there are *multiple* correct answers to most problems, and I trust myself to choose well and choose faster."

Let Go Of Anxiety—Anxiety is fear that has no source—it's worrying "just in case." Anxiety really fills up a closet fast.
Replace with: "I know that things may go wrong, and I trust that I am smart enough and capable enough to figure out what to do when that happens. Meanwhile, I refuse to waste my energy on something that does not exist."

Let Go Of Needing To Be Right—The extra energy required to win *every* conversation *every* time drains you more than you realize.
Replace with: "I am open to others' good ideas. I speak up when I have a concern, and as long as I feel that I am heard, I'm okay with the final outcome."

Let Go Of Resentment—Carrying resentment around is like drinking poison and expecting the other person to die. Holding on to old wrongs is like setting a moth colony loose on your wool sweater collection and then hating your grandma for knitting.
Replace with: "I forgive you. I cannot forget what you did or what happened to me, but I will no longer allow that to control me. I take back my own power to control my life from today forward."

Let Go Of Hatred And Intolerance—Disliking and disagreeing with others can sometimes help us feel better about ourselves, but only to the extent that we are able to tear others down so they are lower than us. Such emotions feel very powerful, yet are always corrosive. They kill us from the inside out. *Replace with:* "I'm not weird—I'm just not you. You're not weird—you're just not me" (Yes, this sounds simple—and I encourage you to try it on and notice what happens when you wear it!).

Let Go Of Impatience—Yes, it is all about you, and *they* are trying to make your life difficult. *They* are deliberately slow to irritate you. *They* purposely messed up your account to waste your time. Sound familiar? *Replace with:* <<Breathe in, deeply. Breathe out, slowly. Repeat>> "I am sure you are trying your best. I am calm as I ask for your help to resolve this issue." <<keep breathing, deeply>>

Let Go Of Being A Know It All—One of the biggest barriers to learning is, "I already know that." When we tell ourselves "this is nothing new" we stop listening and we stop learning; and when we stop learning, we stop growing; and when we stop growing… we die. *Replace with:* "I am always learning. I am open to new ideas, perspectives, and possibilities. Even if I heard this before, I am in a different place today, and I know that I will find deeper meaning than I did last time I heard it."

Let Go Of Unhappiness—Some amount of discontent with the status quo can serve to drive you. When you find yourself constantly unhappy with today, though, it's time to try on a different outfit. *Replace with:* "I choose to enjoy where I am today, even as I aspire to something else. My life is not perfect and I am flawed, *and* that means that I am a perfectly normal human being."

Applying the Skill: *Step One:* Pick a day or week for this project, and circle it on your calendar. When the day arrives, put on your Closet Cleaning outfit—something that makes you feel powerful— and have a copy of the above checklist handy. Start by pitching what no longer makes you feel fabulous.

Step Two: As you sort through those comfortable old emotions, treat them with respect. Listen to the story that goes with each one. Savor the memories connected to the items—you've kept them in your closet for a reason. Tell the story one last time, and then decide what would better serve you. Let the old outfit go to make space for happiness and new positive stories.

Step Three: Repeat annually.

~~☺~~☺~~☺~~☺~~

In the Workplace: Same Rules Apply

The above exercise also applies to your workplace—except that at work we keep stuff in a drawer or overhead cabinet rather than a closet. Purge your workspace regularly, too.

When you're comfortable with letting go, share your skill and experience with others who have difficulty with it. When you hear someone say, "that's how we've always done it," or "that's the way I was taught," realize that you have an opportunity to mentor someone who may have problems with change. Encourage them to tell you their story, and help them to replace that story with one about the future that is full of hope and possibility.

So remember...

LEADERSHIP IS NOT ABOUT A TITLE...	ANYONE CAN BE A LEADER WHO HELPS OTHERS LET GO OF WHAT WAS, IN ORDER TO ENJOY WHAT IS YET TO COME

My Own Chair!

Just about everything in our environment can hold an emotional tale. My mother has in her living room an antique, wrap-around armchair covered in green velveteen that is ugly, uncomfortable as heck, and actually dangerous to small children. Yet she will not give it up because it was her mother's, and because it was one of the last pieces of furniture my dad reupholstered (his hobby) before he died two decades ago.

Furniture and environment, like our clothes, can play with our emotions. Here's a story about my own relationship with furniture:

I was one of eight kids in my family. Growing up in a crowded, crazy home, everything was community property. I watched TV shows where the dad came home to a calm house, sat down in *his* chair, and read the paper. It seemed like he relaxed in that chair all evening, and I thought, "Someday, that will be me."

When Cheryl and I were married right out of college, we furnished our apartment—and later our own home—with hand-me-downs that served us well and were functional...but not necessarily comfortable. By the time we had funds to upgrade our living room furniture, we were expanding our own family, so everything we purchased was rated for durability and its capacity to hold a crowd.

As our four kids grew, our furniture choices focused on everyone having their own space (to reduce arguing!). We spent a lot of years with two large couches as our primary furniture, so everyone had a reserved space but no one really had their own chair, no, not even Dad. I compromised to keep peace in the family...

Several years later when our daughter and new son-in-law set up their house with a brand new living room set, Cheryl fell totally in love with their overstuffed recliner. When she and I walked back into our own house (next door ☺) and looked at the two, ten-year-old couches that dominated our living room, we realized that we were so ready to part with the past. I mean, we only had one child left at home, and he spent 80% of his time at school—why was our house still set up to accommodate six? So, we sold half of our living room to a second-hand store then went out and purchased two pieces of furniture.

We felt so wicked! We had to custom-order the fabric we wanted, so for eight weeks we have had just one piece of furniture in our living room. We did set up a couple of folding chairs for guests, but wow!—the room felt so big and empty!

The new furniture arrived, including an overstuffed, rocking lounger for Cheryl and a big recliner for me. Actually, it's called a "chair and a half" and it is one huge piece of furniture. I can sit cross-legged or lie back and spread out... and it is all *mine*. I love this chair!

You may think I'm being silly, and maybe I am. So? If I haven't earned the right to be a little silly by now, then when? I'm in my 50s now, and for the first time in my life I have my very own, no-compromise, don't-have-to-share-it-with-anyone-else chair. And I feel wickedly happy!

Practice #3—Appreciate All Emotions, In Balance

Occasionally, I have a conversation with someone who is uncomfortable talking about Happiness. They hear my title and immediately back away as though I have a contagious virus. Once, a person waved me away and said, "Frankly, I don't want to be happy all the time, Jim." Honestly, neither do I. Just to put this in perspective, let's step away from Happiness and talk about the value in other emotions.

Is Happiness a Good Thing?

My work is not about achieving endless bliss, nirvana, seventh heaven, or whatever you choose to call it. It is about knowing how to: 1.) Experience and enjoy happiness; then, 2.) Revisit that emotional realm at will and not have it be distant or unattainable.

My work is about helping people realize they have choices about the emotions they feel, and then to teach them how to make those choices differently (e.g., Happiness is a decision...). So, can you be *too* happy? Yes. Consider this definition of happiness: "The quality or state of being joyous, glad, or contented." I'm sure you all want joy in your lives, but if that's the only place you lived, would you appreciate it as much?

~~☺~~☺~~☺~~☺~~

Discontent Drives Progress

If you were content all the time, you might lose all your motivation to do better, to move ahead, to learn, and to grow. In fact, some studies have found that people who report consistently high levels of happiness, e.g., 9 or 10 on a 10-point scale, achieve less in school and career environments when compared to those who come in at 7 or 8 on the same scale.

To be fair, one can argue that if a person says they're at a 10 on the happiness scale, isn't that the ultimate achievement? I mean, if Chris makes $35K a year and is perfectly happy in his job and his lot in life, would he ever need to make more money or have a new job? Probably not, and good for him!

If everyone felt like Chris, we would never have left the caves thousands of years ago. The fact is that without some amount of UNhappiness and DIScontentment, we wouldn't have all the wonderful things that make life interesting, like electric light bulbs, air flight, chocolate ice cream, calculators, and the internet. Think about it—innovation only occurs when someone wants something MORE than what is. Would we have spaghetti with Marinara sauce today if a few Italian explorers hadn't been a little restless (Marco Polo brought the secret of noodle making from China to Italy and Christopher Columbus brought tomatoes from the Americas)? Would Thomas Edison have kept trying to perfect the light bulb after 100, 300, or 500+ failures if he was satisfied with the gas lighting of his day?

~~☺~~☺~~☺~~☺~~

All Emotions, In Balance

In fact, every human emotion serves a purpose. *Fear* kept us from being eaten by saber-tooth tigers. *Frustration* keeps us from spending too much time in unresolved situations. *Disgust* is a survival emotion that prevents us from eating moldy food or other things that could make us sick. *Caution* stops us from stepping off the sidewalk in front of speeding traffic or from signing legal papers without reading them first.

Lest I be misunderstood, let me clarify—Happiness is a good thing. I *want* more happiness in my life, and I'm guessing you do, too. Let's just make sure happiness and optimism are mixed with appropriate amounts of ambition for the future, desire for learning, and justifiable anger when someone harms us. Just as in nearly every other area of life, balance and moderation are best.

A main 'Criteria of Consciousness' for the human experience is never having all you want. For as one dream comes true, another swiftly takes its place. Not having all you want is one of life's constants. And learning to be happy while not yet having all you want (which, as you can see, is constant), is the first 'Criteria of Joy.' Nail it, and for the rest of your life people will be asking what it is about you.
~~from "Messages from the Universe" at www.Tut.com

Applying the Skill: On a sheet of paper, draw a line down the center. On one side, make a quick list of the conditions in your life that are positive and about which you are happy. On the other, make a quick list of the conditions in your life you wish to change.

Now step back and notice how you are able to experience happiness with some aspects of your life even as you hold a degree of discontent with others. Take a moment to express gratitude for both lists—the things that bring you happiness and the things that keep you learning, growing, and experiencing more of life.

If you ache to do something with your lists, try this: Use the tally of Positives to jump start your Joy List (discussed under Principle 3, Live for Life, Not Stuff) or add to one that's already in process. For the conditions you'd like to change, move a few to your current task list or onto your Tolerations List (see Principle 6, Tolerate Nothing) where you will take action to open up more space for happiness

~~☺~~☺~~☺~~☺~~

Mostly Happy—But Not Always!

The following concept is proven by research and is almost universally accepted—happy employees work harder, are more creative, solve problems faster, are sick less often, and engage more fully. To wit—happier employees support a better bottom line.

71

Yet do we want employees who are always happy, never discontent? Not really. We want innovation (which requires a desire for improvement), constructive conflict (which arises from ambition), prudence with financial and material resources (requiring caution and concern), and continual learning (which comes from wanting more and better).

Leaders must learn how to nurture an environment that appropriately balances gratitude for past contribution and the demand for more and better next time. Only when we balance contentment and discontent can we create a happy *and* ambitious workplace.

So remember...

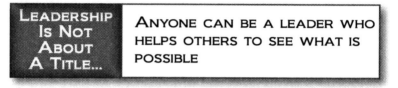

LEADERSHIP IS NOT ABOUT A TITLE... ANYONE CAN BE A LEADER WHO HELPS OTHERS TO SEE WHAT IS POSSIBLE

Practice #4—Pay Attention to What You Take In: Detox, Oprah, And The Search For Chocolate

Not long ago, my digestive system was acting up. I won't trouble you with symptoms—but I tell you that my doctor wanted to put me on medication. I resist taking pills—I hate the side effects. The only pills I want to take are vitamins and an occasional pain reliever. So I opted to try a different approach: if eating is what caused my issues, what if I changed what and how I eat?

I planned to implement a detoxification diet; first, I would eliminate a lot of different foods, then gradually put them back one at a time until I could discover what was causing my system to go all nasty on me. My plan looked like this:

- No animal products (meats, eggs, milk, cheese, etc.)
- No sugars (other than naturally occurring, as in fruit)
- No alcohol
- No caffeine
- No glutens (no bread, nothing with wheat, etc.)

My wife's reaction was, "What's left?!" I sensed her skepticism. The next day she came back to me and announced, "Oprah said she's doing a 21-day Cleanse. I checked her website, and I think it's the same thing you want to do." Suddenly, I had Cheryl's support *plus* an entire website of recipes created by Oprah's personal chef. How cool is that? Timing is everything, right?

Turns out that, even after eliminating those five food groups, *a lot* was left. I ate like a vegan for three weeks, cooking up some amazing dishes. I learned how to make sesame tahini, hummus, and baba ghanoush from scratch, to turn tofu and rice noodles into a gourmet meal, mixed up a fabulous fat-free granola, and transformed beans into an incredible minestrone by adding fresh veggies and quinoa noodles.

Cheryl opted not to participate in the no-wheat/no-meat part of the detox, but did share my salad regimen. We explored all sorts of greens (arugula, red leaf, mustard & beet greens, spinach, and dandelion leaves) and tossed in whatever we had in the house: strawberries, blueberries, tomatoes, cooked rice, pumpkin seeds, coconut… added a drizzle of olive oil, and we had a meal.

The big obstacle for me was the lack of chocolate, but I didn't give up. I figured out that a teaspoon of cocoa powder mixed with a half cup of soy yogurt and some sliced strawberries is a lovely dessert. After all, this was about diet, not denial, right?! To be honest, I was miserable for the first five days, falling asleep at my desk, craving sweets, and feeling icky. Then, like flipping a switch, it all stopped. For the next 2.5 weeks I felt fabulous! So much so that I was reluctant to go back to my normal cuisine. I was more alert, slept better, and my digestive system seemed to work perfectly, and I had no interest in sweets. I found this all to be fascinating.

~~☺~~☺~~☺~~☺~~

You Are What You Eat—Physically and Emotionally

The most amazing outcome of all was how much attention I paid to everything I put in to my body—and the realization that I was not paying attention before. They say, "You Are What You Eat," and I now 'get' that in a whole new way.

It also caused me to reflect on what I put into my emotional self—my self-talk, what I read, what I watched on TV, the conversations I held. When I'm taking in negativity, stress, and bad news, I feel like crap. It's hard to feel upbeat and happy if I am immersed in a downer environment or if I'm focused on my shortcomings instead of my accomplishments. Now, what might a *21-day emotional cleanse* look like. Perhaps this?

- No negative self-talk
- No gossip, or complaining
- No making promises I can't keep
- No mainstream media (no war, politics, murder, etc.)
- No downer conversations with people who carry negative attitudes
- Focus daily on what I *did* vs. what I *did not* do

Tips & Tools

Applying the Skill: Think about what you want to eliminate from your *emotional diet* for 21 days; you can start with the ideas above. Write those down and share the list—and your challenge—with friends and family. Post the list where you'll see it often.

Obtain a large, wide rubber band that will fit comfortably around your wrist without restricting circulation. Whenever you or others notice that you are engaging in one of the activities on your list, give the rubber band a good hard snap. Ouch, that stings! The physical sensation will serve to reinforce that you do NOT want to do that again.

Try to go an entire day without having to snap the rubber band. Be patient with yourself—these behaviors are entrenched, and you'll make mistakes. Forgive yourself and start over.

Once you've gone a day, go for two. Work yourself up gradually. When you can go three to four weeks without engaging in any of those toxic emotional activities, give yourself a reward. You'll be well on your way to some wonderful new emotional habits.

~~☺~~☺~~☺~~☺~~

And speaking of Chocolate...

Spreadable Chocolate

 Hello, my name is Jim, and I am a chocoholic. Please keep that in mind as you read this. My eldest daughter Kelly and her fiancé drove from Philadelphia to North Carolina to join us on our beach vacation. Tucked into their food bag was an odd little plastic container filled with a brown gel. "Here, Dad, you should try this," she urged.

Four years before, Kelly spent her junior year in college abroad in Europe. There, she discovered a European grocery staple and source of protein. It is made with ground hazelnuts, skim milk, and cocoa. They carried it with them everywhere on their travels. It is relatively inexpensive, easy to transport, requires no refrigeration, and can serve as a meal supplement, a meal-on-the-run (spread on bread or crackers), or as a dessert.

So, I tried it. It was smooth and had the consistency of peanut butter … yet the taste was definitely chocolate! Soft, satiny, spreadable, dark chocolate.

Oh, my goodness! This certainly put a smile on my face! I rationed the half jar they left with me, one tablespoon a day for the remainder of our vacation. I mixed it with strawberries, fresh peaches, spread it on warm rye toast, melted it into hot coffee, spread it on a chocolate-chip cookie and even, when I felt especially wicked, ate it plain.

Have you ever plunged a spoon into the peanut-butter jar and then stuck it in your mouth? Imagine that peanut-butter feel—it sticks to the roof of your mouth and coats your tongue and you have to lick the spoon repeatedly to get off every last little bit because you don't want to waste any of it. And now, imagine that it is not peanut butter you taste, but dark chocolate. Ooooh! ☺ The product and my new addiction is called Nutella. It's in the peanut butter-and-jelly section in the grocery store. Enjoy!

Practice #5—Do A Teardown And Rebuild Of Your Life: Nine Lessons From A House

Following a series of conversations over several years, my wife and I became real estate investors. We purchased the house next to ours from its original owners, who had it built in 1955. They loved that house when they moved into it over 50 years ago—so much so that they kept it exactly the way it was. The walls were the original color, the original stove still cooked their food, and … well, you get the idea. The house has good bones but it was several decades overdue for some serious updating. And painting—*lots of painting*. So we immersed ourselves in a complete overhaul of the property. Once completed, we planned to make it a rental property, and our first tenant was our daughter and her husband following their wedding.

This was a huge project—walls were moved; the kitchen was torn down to the studs; we rewired the entire house; replaced every appliance, window, door, light, sink, faucet, and floor covering. Whatever was left, we stained or painted. It was still the same house, yet it will never be the same as it was (and the better for it).

That latter sentiment got me to thinking about how this house makeover holds many lessons for people who seek to do the same renovation for their lives.

Nine Lessons Learned From A House

#1. *Work on your wiring, first.* Renovating a house wired for 1950s electrical needs, our first priority was to upgrade the infrastructure. Today's twenty- and thirty-somethings are always plugged in, so this meant we had to rewire the house to fit the increased electrical demands of our tenants' Millennial lifestyle (e.g., laptops in every room, big-screen LCD TV, programmable coffee maker, etc.) or they would blow the electrical grid.

So too, the first step in personal change is often a rewiring of self-talk and personal practices. Perhaps you need to change the stories you tell yourself about yourself; or shift some physical practice or attitude that no longer serves you. When you shift the flow of positive energy in your system, you're more likely to have the capacity to handle what life throws at you.

#2. *Get rid of the old junk.* The prior owners left a lot of stuff in the house. I'm sure that if we'd really tried, we could have found an antiques lover or dealer who'd have swooned over a 1955 electric stove with all the original components. But in the end, to us, it was just old, tired junk—it all had to go.

Do you hang on to old ideas, thoughts, and practices sometimes beyond their usefulness? If you ever hear yourself say things like, "in the old days..." or "that's not how we used to do it..." you may be dealing in antiquated thinking. Help yourself to focus on the way things are now, and pitch what is no longer useful. You'll love the space that opens up in your life for happiness.

#3. *Envisioning the future is easier once you remove what's in the way.* The rooms in the house looked so small until we removed all the junk. Until we actually tore down the kitchen wall, no one could picture the larger space that was possible. Once we removed the obstacles, it became immensely easier to stand in the space and imagine the future.

I've worked with clients who remain stuck not because they lack motivation but because they can't picture where they're going. So we seek to remove barriers first—old perspectives, assumptions, and habits. Only then do we try to define the future. What's in your way that you might remove?

#4. *Sometimes, less is more.* Fifty years of benign neglect in the yard meant that anything that started to grow...grew. We cut down five decades of overgrowth, and pruned back 80% of the trees and shrubs. The simplified landscape has drawn dozens of positive comments from the neighbors, most of whom had never seen the front of the house.

Maybe you've allowed some of your habits to grow unchecked over several decades until they hide parts of you. What would emerge if you *pruned away* one or two of those things you've been doing/thinking the same way since high school? Any trained landscaper will tell you a healthy pruning is not about cutting away, it's about opening up space for new growth. So let go of an old habit, reaction, or opinion. You might discover a part of you that surprises!

#5. *A fresh coat of paint can work miracles.* 50% of the house front was covered in dark brown siding. After two coats of light green paint, the house literally leapt from the shadows to claim a proud new position in the neighborhood.

What can you do to touch up your exterior? Consider the power of a smile. We catch our emotions from others—and when one person shows up with a smile on his or her face, the emotional contagion can ripple across a room in minutes. Putting on a different face can be just as transforming as a paint job, for a heck of a lot less work!

#6. *Take Before and After pictures to really appreciate your progress.* Despite a month's hard work, the interior of the house still looked far from livable. In the moments of discouragement, we turned to the pictures I took the day after we got the keys. Quickly, we appreciated our progress and returned to the project with greater optimism.

When you strive to change a habit, there will be lots of days when you feel like you're in the same place as always. To help you along, take time before you start to create a "picture" of the old You. Maybe that's an actual photo; or perhaps it's an assessment, a checklist, or a letter to yourself that details your starting point. Then use that to boost your spirits and remind yourself of the progress you've made since you started your journey.

#7. *Ask for help—it's there.* As we began this huge project—on our own—we assumed we'd be making it up as we went. Turned out that many of our friends and neighbors were also excited by our project and incredibly eager to help us out. Some lent us equipment, some their expertise, and others gave moral support, all of which helped.

When you seek to shift a behavior, habit, or attitude, do you think, "I have to do this myself"? Sharing a goal with others can often generate more ideas and create an unexpected network of support. Friends like to help friends.

#8. *Don't be afraid to be bold.* During our planning discussions, many ideas were tossed about, from combining rooms to designer kitchens to painting a 12'-high wall dark purple. Because we entertained the ideas, the final plan—while mostly conventional—included several splashes of excitement!

When it comes to living a happier life, consider this: If you continue to do what you've always done (the "safe" route), you'll end up exactly where you are. What shift in thinking or habit would, for you, be the equivalent of painting one of your walls bright purple?

#9. *The plan is ALWAYS evolving.* We had to redraw the kitchen plans several times—wiring here won't work that way; this wall won't support the extra weight; standard cabinets don't come in that size, and so on. Each time we redesigned for something we *couldn't* have, we found that new options often improved the final design.

The only thing certain about the future is that it will turn out differently than expected. Above all, a personal plan for change requires flexibility. Don't get married to the details; rather, fall in love with the *concept*, and remember that there are multiple, *multiple* paths to more happiness in your life!

Applying the Skill: Pick one of the above lessons and consider how you can apply it to your life or work. For one week, focus on removing, adding, or putting a new face on some part of you, and then pay attention to how your *neighbors* respond to your *remodeling*. Above all, have fun!

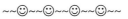

In The Workplace: Build A Strong Foundation

Have you ever watched a house or an office building under construction? At first, there is an endless period when nothing seems to happen, then all of a sudden—WHAM—the frame is up; workers swarm all over and before you know it the grass is planted and moving trucks are backing in to unload.

We all know someone who moved into a new home and then discovered, to his or her chagrin, that the basement leaked or a wall was cracking. What happened? The builder took shortcuts on the foundation so, despite the beautiful yard and the designer kitchen, the new owner has to spend all their time downstairs bailing water, or outside digging up the landscape to fix what should have been done earlier.

No matter where you work, there's probably some level of building or remodeling going on—change is a constant! When you are in a leadership position, you have a choice every day about how you spend your time. You likely have multiple projects to work on or oversee, meetings to plan or attend, calls to take and make, and endless emails to process. And you have all those people out there. You really should get out there and talk with them to see how and what they are doing. But hey, the boss left a voicemail seeking a project status update and no one is asking whether you've energized your staff today. So, call the boss back and handle some more emails, right?

Well, if you want a smooth rollout, you need your team on board. And they are far more likely to work with you—through all the issues that arise from the current remodeling—if they like you, trust you, and believe you care about them and understand their situation.

If you want to build a reputation for getting things done, you must spend time up front engaged in activities that do not show up on a project plan. There is no substitute for real people having real conversations with real people. This is how a real leader builds strong foundations for future change.

So remember...

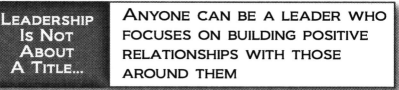

LEADERSHIP IS NOT ABOUT A TITLE... ANYONE CAN BE A LEADER WHO FOCUSES ON BUILDING POSITIVE RELATIONSHIPS WITH THOSE AROUND THEM

Practice #6—Thanksgetting: The Skill Of Accepting Gratitude

The saying goes, "It is better to give then receive." We spend a lot of time focused on giving thanks and sharing gratitude. Many countries even have a holiday dedicated to gratitude (e.g., Thanksgiving in the US and Canada). Yet *giving* is only 50% of a transaction; so let's look at the *receiving* end of the process.

I have a good friend who is impossible to praise. If I say, "I really appreciate all the hard work you put into this project," she says, "Thank you for saying that." If I say, "I think you look fantastic today!" She says, "Thank you for saying that." Do you see my concern? Here am I, taking the time to share my appreciation or a compliment, and her words and tone declare, "I don't believe you mean what you say. You're only saying it to make me feel better, but thanks anyway for saying it. Can we talk about something else?!"

My experience is like that of someone who has taken the time to select, wrap, and deliver a gift that the embarrassed recipient then takes and places into a closet, which is full of other unwrapped gifts. Hey, what about *opening* the gift? If you don't open my gift, I feel like I've been denied the joy of giving. The gratitude was acknowledged but not accepted.

Do you know anyone like this? Actually, you do, me. In early 2004, I first became aware that I deflect praise and gratitude. Pay me a compliment? I'd explain that it was "the team." Say you admire my skill or delivery in a program? I'd talk about how the group was unusually cooperative. Tell me you were grateful for my help in resolving a problem? I'd tell you I got lucky that day. I had no idea that I was effectively dissing those who were trying to share their gratitude with me.

Then one day I found myself being confronted by a man who refused to let me walk away from the conversation. "I'm not feeling heard," he said. "I just shared with you my admiration for what you did, and you just blew me off." What was this guy talking about?

It turns out, he was right. I learned then, and many other times since, that I have trouble accepting gratitude, praise, compliments, and admiration. I mean, the sound comes in to my eardrums, but I don't always HEAR and accept the gratitude. I had to learn to stop, make eye contact, feel the gratitude in my body as a physical sensation and say, simply, "Thank you." Thank you. Period. Not, *thankyouverymuch*, or *itwasnothingreally*, or *pleasedon'tmentionit...* blah, blah, blah.

So, I've been working on this new way of receiving gratitude and praise, this "new body," if you will. And I've had some wonderful conversations that would not have opened up if I'd showed up in my old habits. Yet still, those old habits die hard.

~~☺~~☺~~☺~~☺~~

Sharing Stories

First story: My younger brother, Kevin, owns a business in Pittsburgh called Elite Runners and Walkers, selling high-quality shoes and running gear to professional & recreational runners (5K, marathoners, etc). He is also a huge supporter and fund raiser for Team In Training, an organization that raises funds through running events to fund leukemia research and provide support for families struggling with that cancer. We lost our youngest brother Sean to leukemia in 1995 when he was 25, and Kevin's life has been inspired by that loss.

I received a wonderful letter from Kevin who wrote to share his joy at having been named one of the Top 50 Best Running Shops in the USA (out of ~500), an honor that is in part based on his community activity and his philanthropy. Wow. AND he wrote to thank me for the influence I've had on his life. He actually credited me with being a part of his success. At first I did not know how to react to his note. I thought about writing him a lovely note of congratulations on his achievement. Period.

After the note sat for a day on my desk, however, I realized that it had probably taken Kevin a bit of courage to write me such a personal and deeply felt letter, and I needed to hear what he was saying to me: Thanks, big brother!

My response to Kevin was full of pride AND acceptance. I felt honored by his letter, and I hope he felt honored by my response.

Second story: I attended a three-day conference to complete my coaching training through the Newfield Network. I had joined this wonderful, international learning community in 2005, and it had been awhile since I last saw my classmates. On the final day of the conference, Angela, a brilliant and sensitive woman from Columbia, came to me and said, "I need to talk with you. Why did you run away from me before? I told you I want to thank you."

Two days earlier, we'd had conversation that I thought was complete. Angela did not feel it was complete. She had not felt HEARD in that conversation. She forced me to look in her eyes as she told me that what I had helped her learn, in a coaching exercise during our previous training session months before, had changed her life.

I remembered the moment. Angela lives in a South American culture that does not traditionally value women, and she carried that with her all the time. I had helped her to learn to declare, in her head, heart, and body, "I am a strong and confident woman." We actually shifted how she stood and walked so that the statement felt more true for her. Apparently, this new way of being and this new declaration rocked her world.

As we talked, I felt Angela's gratitude wash over me like an ocean wave. It was warm and powerful. And she said, with a big smile, "I think you get what I'm saying. Now, I feel heard."

So now when the holidays come around each year, I practice both Thanks GIVING as well as Thanks GETTING.

 Applying the Skill: Consider how you accept gratitude. Do you "open the gift" by accepting it gracefully, allowing the giver to participate in the gift giving? Or do you set it aside for later, or reject it altogether, tossing it in your closet, unopened? For the next few weeks, pay attention to how you handle thanks and gratitude. When someone thanks you, instead of lobbing a quick *oh, you're welcome* or *it'snothing,don'tmentionit* at them, stop for a moment, smile, and look into their eyes. Say, carefully and from your heart, "You are welcome." Or, "It was my pleasure."

And when someone expresses praise, appreciation, or shares a compliment with you, take a deep breath; breathe that appreciation into the core of your body and pause a moment to *feel* as well as *hear* what is being said. Feel the smile emerge on your face. Accept the gift, unwrap it, and see that gift through the eyes of the person who picked it out especially for you, who so carefully wrapped it and made a point of delivering it to you. Show respect for the person who did the giving. Get the thanks, and honor the act of giving, then simply say, "Thank you."

Practice #7—Give More Than "Just Enough"

 You've likely seen one of the many workplace surveys done in recent years that tell us 67% of employees say they have received no positive feedback or appreciation in the past year.

Is this real? Two thirds of the workforce has heard nothing in an entire year, not even a simple thank you? I truly believe most managers when they say that they give positive feedback, and that they are frustrated that people don't hear that feedback. Yet, the numbers are the numbers.

I might ask a manager, "How do you give that feedback? When do you give that feedback? And how often?" "I just told them in their last review!" is the typical response. When *before* that? A quiet pause, and a shrugging of shoulders, "I'm not sure. But I'm sure there were at least a couple times…"

Well, there you go. It's not that people are lying when they say they have received no appreciation in the past year—it's just that they truly can't remember, because it was too little for the incident(s) to register in their system. Or worse, the one or two pieces of positive feedback they received were sandwiched around (or immediately followed by) statements of criticism, disappointment, or messages that said, "you're not cutting it." No wonder they have no recollection of positive!

Think about it: if you received only one favorable e-mail each year and every other day you received nothing but reminders of deadlines, notes about errors, and anonymous junk mail, you'd probably carry around a generally negative view of email with no memory of "that one time I got a good one…."

In order for people (and this includes coworkers, children, partners, and friends) to hear gratitude, you must offer enough volume of it, frequently enough, and with specifics, such that they can hear you over the static of the daily routine. Studies tell us that appreciation does not register until the ratio of positive to negative hits at least 3:1 (three positive to every one "corrective" piece of feedback). In other words, if others are not *getting* the thanks and appreciation you offer, consider how you are *giving* it.

Tips & Tools

Applying the Skill: Start by increasing awareness of what feedback you offer and how often you do so. Here is an idea for increasing awareness that can you can use at the workplace and at home:

The Four Quarters Technique. This is a simple and effective tool for shifting your awareness. Start off each morning with four quarters in your right pocket. Each time you offer thanks or praise to a member of your team, transfer one coin from right to left. You cannot leave the office at the end of your shift until you've moved all four quarters to your other pocket.

Options:

- If you are rusty at offering thanks, track your progress on a checklist or spreadsheet to make sure you spread your efforts evenly.

- If someone on the team is not performing well, you may have to look hard for occasions to praise or offer thanks… look hard anyway. Sometimes the main drain on someone's performance is the belief that no one cares what he or she does. You have the power to change that perspective.

- What if you have a small team, and you're afraid of "over doing" the praise thing? Use the four quarters as a reminder to have a personal interaction with at least four people everyday. While people want appreciation, what they want even more is your *attention*.

- If you have a large team it will take longer to circulate among all the players. Unless you have over 80 members on your team, those four 'thank you' interactions every day will mean every person on your team feels a little gratitude at least once a month, which is 12 times/year. If they currently get zero from you, 12 is infinitely better!

- Instead of quarters, substitute any object in fours. One client chose four plastic ducks that she moved from one side of her computer to the other each day. Another put four dark chocolate kisses on his desk and ate one each time he offered thanks. As a side benefit, he lost weight—seriously! He used to snack indiscriminately from candy jars, but when he began the Four Kiss technique, he stopped all snacking except when he earned it for himself.

Use The Four Quarters Technique At Home. With a few twists, this simple tool can quickly change the culture of a family. Instead of quarters in a pocket, you can use stuffed animals on a shelf or magnets on the fridge. Engage the entire family, where the goal is for every person in the family to have four gratitude conversations each day or week. Or you can require that parents only get to transfer a quarter when their conversation lasts five minutes or longer. Include spouses as well as kids in the exercise. Then watch what happens when the entire family is practicing gratitude and thanks!

So remember...

 **ANYONE CAN BE A LEADER WHO TAKES TIME TO SAY, "THANK YOU. I APPRECIATE WHAT YOU DID!"**

Practice #8—Smile: Happiness Is Not A Spectator Sport

Reflection

Mood and emotion:
We get back what we send out.
We are all mirrors.

There was a sign at the bottom of the bathroom mirror in the beach front cottage where we spent our vacation. Applied with an old plastic label maker, the corners turning up after decades of washing, it read:

GOOD MORNING!
I WILL BE WITH YOU ALL DAY.
SO PLEASE SMILE!

"How cool is this?" I thought, "Here I am, the Happiness Coach, and I get assigned the Happy Bathroom!" The sign reminded me that smiling serves *me* as much, if not more than, it serves anyone else. My decision to smile, to be happy, to live in a happy body, to carry a happy mood, etc., predisposes me to respond to situations in a very different way than if I decide to carry a frown or to make no conscious effort to carry myself in any particular way at all.

We are emotional animals and, whether we realize or not, we are putting out and receiving hundreds/thousands of non-verbal emotional cues all day and are constantly adjusting to others. So if you want to change your mood, hang around with people who already know how to live where you want to be. Think about it, if you hate the cold, would you want to live in Minnesota or Maine? They can be beautiful places but they have colder weather 8 out of 12 months.

Want to increase your happiness? Emotional resiliency? Calm centeredness? Ability to listen? Then choose an environment where the people live the way you want to live, too. Hang around people who are happier, more resilient, more centered, or better listeners than you.

The information base we get from reading or training is only part of what's required for change. The rest is a complex network of limbic (emotional) signals that can only be learned—often without conscious thinking—in interaction with others, learning and practicing the skills, reading body language, and paying attention to the emotional signals sent/received by others.

This is why the decision to smile is important. It will affect interactions, reactions, and learning. Ever been in a meeting and the convener stomps into the room, plops his or her things down and begins the meeting immediately. His or her negative mood sweeps through the room like a tsunami. Ever been in a meeting where the convener walks in, cheerfully says good morning? What does everyone do, instinctively? They all say "Good morning!" and the meeting begins cheerfully. Really! The decision to smile can improve the mood of individuals, teams, groups, departments, and whole companies! Happiness is not a spectator sport.

Applying the Skill: Smile more—this is an exercise quite simple in concept that can require substantial effort to pull off. Basically: Get up tomorrow and decide that you are going to project a smile all day. Oh, I see. Well, yes, I hear that you have lots of problems. OK, maybe you are having a bad day. At a minimum, then, double the amount of smiling that might occur to you normally. What's that? Still too tough? You say that your cheeks hurt when you smile? Then you need to do this for at least a week! Remember that little poem at the top of this section? The one that said we are all mirrors? If you claim that no one in your world smiles, then consider what you are putting out there. Try this for a few days and notice what happens. If you do it, I'll bet you will notice a lot more happy faces in your world!

~~☺~~☺~~☺~~☺~~

Cause And Consequence

A smile is both a cause and a consequence of workplace happiness. The consequence part is easy—a smile is the universal sign that one is experiencing a good feeling. So smiling in the workplace can tell us much about mood and morale.

Just as babies look to their parents to learn to sync up and tune their emotional responses and behavior, so too do adults in the workplace look to more experienced coworkers (especially their boss) to tune up mood and behavior on the job. Unfortunately, many managers approach moving through the workspace like a nervous tourist visiting New York City: "Keep your head down! Don't make eye contact or they might ask you for something!"

The reality is that if you wear a smile, even in New York City, you'll see a lot more smiling faces looking back at you. And the leader who makes eye contact and carries a genuine smile as they move through the workspace is perceived as more trustworthy and approachable. Plus, smiling is contagious, and the more it is spread around the office internally, the more often it shows up with customers, in meetings, and in those all important one-on-one conversations that seem to happen more often in a trusting environment.

So remember...

LEADERSHIP IS NOT ABOUT A TITLE...	ANYONE CAN BE A LEADER WHEN THEY FOCUS ON HELPING OTHERS SUCCEED BY PROVIDING A POSITIVE INFLUENCE

Practice #9—Give and Receive HUGs: Human Understanding Given

 Many years ago, when I was a young supervisor, I worked with an older woman named Anna. Anna was the department's designated grandmother—dispensing advice, listening to troubles, and always there with a hug. She taught me that hugs were lifeblood; "A person needs three hugs a day for survival, and twelve a day for growth," she would say. Anna's personal mission was to make sure that everybody got at least one-a-day from her. And what great hugs they were—as her big strong arms wrapped you up, so too did her warm and loving heart. I could rarely escape from one of her hugs, and always felt transformed after receiving one. Thus, Anna is responsible for my outlook on hugs.

When my wife became over stressed as we prepared for our daughter's wedding, renovated a house, worked overtime, and were generally overcommitted, it took a toll on her health. Cheryl was rushed to the Emergency Room from her place of work. Her blood sugar was 41 (that's bad, normal is 70–150) and her blood pressure was 70 over nothing (really bad!). Her doctors filled her up with antibiotics for a minor infection she was carrying at the time, and she returned to her routines in a few days. We thought this was an isolated episode.

However, she continued to be fatigued—unable to sleep at night, then difficulty getting up and functioning the next day, etc. She barely made it through our daughter's bridal shower, and the next day she suddenly collapsed.

Basically, her systems—physical and emotional—all shut down. No appetite, no sleep, nausea 24/7, interminable fatigue and physical weakness, feelings of depression and anxiety, disorientation, fuzzy vision.... And to make matters worse, she had reactions to some of the sleep aids our doctor prescribed, so it was a week before she was able to sleep.

We were incredibly frustrated, as her symptoms could arise from a dozen different causes. So figuring out how to treat her was a process of "diagnosis by exclusion," meaning that we started with obvious stuff and started ruling things out.

After many tests (and a lot of blood draws) her doctor was able to rule out a series of possible physical illnesses. What emerged as the primary diagnosis is that she *decompensated* (yes, it's a real word!) In psychological terms it means: The inability to maintain defense mechanisms in response to stress. Plainly stated, she worked herself into a place of extreme mental exhaustion in response to stress, and her emotional system collapsed, taking the physical along with it.

We learned that it wasn't just short-term stress that incapacitated Cheryl; it was actually several issues that built up over several years; it had taken her a long time to stress out and it would take a long time and much support for her to come back. Therefore, in addition to the doctor's prescribed recovery plan, I decided that I would incorporate a 12-a-day hug strategy as an important part of Cheryl's recovery. Though she had not previously bought into my "touchy-feely" profession, she now, according to her doctor, had to change how she managed stress. Luckily for her, she was married to a Happiness Coach!

Six-weeks later, as we stood in the receiving line at our daughter's wedding, I watched as many of our friends and family used the opportunity to give Cheryl some extra big hugs. So glad they were to see her well and whole again. Hugs have the power to convey so much love and support, and I found myself thinking about the meaning of the word, hug.

Over the months that followed, as I shared Cheryl's story with friends, clients, and colleagues, I had many people tell me that they, too, tried the 12-hugs-per-day technique. Several of them reported that the exercise was, A) more difficult than expected, and B) a very positive experience.

The *American Heritage Dictionary* defines hug as:

> *v.: To clasp or hold closely, especially in the arms,*
> *as in affection; embrace.*

The etymology of the word is unclear. Perhaps it comes from *hugge* "to embrace," perhaps from the Old Norse *hugga* "to comfort," or *hugr* "courage, mood," or from the Old English *hycgan* "to think, consider," or even the Gothic *hugs* meaning "mind, soul, thought."

I like all of these possible roots. Hugs are certainly about conveying comfort. I believe it often requires courage to offer a hug; hugs can change one's mood, and a good hug can come from—and connect to—one's very soul. A hug is one of the most human things humans do. So I like the definition my wife uses: HUG stands for **H**uman **U**nderstanding **G**iven. Perfect!

When we hug each other, we are in effect saying, "The human being in me connects to the human being in you." And note the form for a good hug:

We face each other, and bring our hearts together. Human. Understanding. Given. What a happy event is a hug….

Applying the Skill: At the end of each year many people experience a higher degree of family, friend, community, or coworker interaction. Chanukah, the Muslim feast of Eid ul-Adha, Christmas, and Kwanzaa are celebrations that bring families together. Holiday gatherings are common, with lots of hugging. Some of it is perfunctory hugging (*do I really have to hug Aunt Mildred?*), which is so unsatisfactory. So try this: The next time someone signals that a hug is imminent (the outstretched arms are usually a signal!), give yourself a treat, and hug back. Just relax and be fully present in that moment, heart to heart. Feel the affection that the other person holds for you, and let them feel the same from you.

In every day there are 20,000 moments.[5] Make your hugs moments that you—and others—will remember.

The Human Touch at Work

In today's hands-off, no-touching, no-hugging workplace, we have this dilemma: we are still all about people connecting with people. How can you communicate human understanding given… without actually hugging?

The good news is that human contact is still necessary and realistic, even in sterile business environments. Some degree of personal touch can be achieved by sticking to safe neutral spots, such as the arms below the shoulders. If you want to congratulate someone on a job well done, you can reach across in a conversation to touch their upper arm or forearm, which will generally not violate any personal space norms, yet still convey a connection. Truly, a warm handshake (clasping with both hands, even) can communicate a lot. And in the absence of any touch, try directly facing the person you are speaking with, and listen attentively. You may not be in physical contact, but you'll still be facing heart to heart, and that sends a non-verbal signal that is both powerful and personal.

So remember...

LEADERSHIP IS NOT ABOUT A TITLE... ANYONE CAN BE A LEADER WHO CREATES A *HUMAN* CONNECTION WITH OTHERS!

Practice #10—Stop Trying So Hard:
Evolve Into Happiness

Human beings are creatures of habit. We draw great comfort from all the little rituals that we build around us—how we brush our teeth, the routes we drive to the places we frequent, the way we prepare the foods we like to eat, the people we hang with, the phrases we use in conversation, and the way we walk, talk, and even breathe.

This tendency to turn everything into a routine is a biologically programmed survival strategy—if early humans had to think about everything, all the time, they would have been so distracted that they would have been easy prey for saber-toothed tigers, and the human race would have died out long ago. So our habits protect us and serve us in many ways. Stability is good for us.

At the same time, that wonderful stabilizing trait gets in the way when we want to change something about ourselves, like, "I want to exercise more. I want to stop procrastinating. I want to be more adventurous. I want to feel more confident, less anxious, more outgoing, more decisive, less aggressive, and on and on. Oh, and happier. I want to feel happier."

Have you ever said any of those things? Trouble is, saying it does not make it so. And living it is a challenge, since your wonderful habits do such a great job of returning you to what you've been doing all along, even if you no longer want to be there, do that, think that, or say that. <Sigh> Why does personal change have to feel so much like hard work?

Hey, stop TRYING so hard. Rather than fighting your human nature, you might try leveraging something else you are really good at: evolving. You are constantly evolving. You are not the same person you were in junior high or at high school graduation or before you had kids or got that promotion or changed jobs. Human beings possess some of the same characteristics as water; we can adapt to the shape of the container in which we are placed.

Once we've adapted, new habits emerge and re-stabilize us. But between the point where our environment shifts and the bureaucracy of habits reestablishes control, we have a window of opportunity. We have the opportunity to *consciously* examine what we do and think and allow ourselves to be pulled into new behaviors and new attitudes.

 Applying the Skill: Select one of the following ideas, or your own version of one, and experiment with it for a couple of weeks to fully experience how your ability to evolve can change your outlook:

1. *Shift something small in your current environment.* Drive a different route to work. Visit a different place of worship to experience a different minister or community (or even just sit in a different pew at your own

place!). Go to lunch with different people. Sit at a different table in the cafeteria and notice what new ideas and conversations you are exposed to. Go to the library and pick up a book from a genre you've never explored. Listen to music from a category you profess to dislike—or in another language! Paint one wall in your living room a vibrant color. Any one of these environmental tweaks holds the potential to challenge and stimulate you. At minimum they might improve your appreciation of what you already have; at best they can expand your world view.

2. ***Shift the people you spend time with.*** Do not underestimate the power of community. If you want to change something about who you are, you can struggle to make a shift through sheer force of personal will (how exhausting!); OR… you can try hanging out with people who already have what you want, rather than people who resemble who you are now.

Want to be happier? Hang out with happy people—they carry a highly infectious 'virus' that you are more likely to pick up if you stay close to them. Aspire to greater creativity? Hang out with the *creatives* (i.e., creative people— artists, musicians, innovators, etc.). Need to think more strategically? Find ways to hang around with and have discussions with other strategic thinkers. When you surround yourself with people who have more of something you want, you'll find it is incredibly easy to change your own thinking or behavior… or happiness!

~~☺~~☺~~☺~~☺~~

Shopping In The House

I am famous in my family for rearranging the furniture, a habit that increased in frequency when I learned that there is an actual home design process called "shopping in the house." I'm constantly moving things to different rooms, to different corners or shelves, etc. One year, for example, I reorganized the pictures on our bookshelf, shuffled where pictures hung on the walls, replaced a rocking chair with a large plant, swapped a table from the bedroom to the living room and vice-versa, and moved lamps around to shift how light fell in the room. The changes refreshed the room and changed the traffic patterns.

I use shopping in the house as a regular strategy. In any given week, I might turn a table on the diagonal, place a pitcher with fresh-cut flowers on the mantle, or shift a couple of room decorations to new locations in the house. These are small things that keep me (and my family) used to small changes and keep us paying attention to the environment. We avoid complacency in our house, and that translates into more energy when we go out into the world.

Plus, the changes always make a room feel fresh and new, without having to paint or buy anything. And that helps me feel happy in my home.

~~☺~~☺~~☺~~☺~~

Shift Your Patterns

For many people, the workplace environment is one where they feel they have little or no control. OK, maybe you are subject to the rules of others and find yourself surrounded by limitations, e.g., you can't change your job duties or the corporate culture. Even so, I encourage you to focus on what you CAN control.

Examine all the patterns and habits you've adopted over time. Do you take your break at the same time, eat lunch with the same people, drive the same route to work, at the same time every day? Do you keep saying the same thing(s) about the company, walk the same route between departments, and attend the same meetings?

Stop it! Select just one of your routines—one of those things you do without much thought—and for a short time, perform it in a different way. Then notice how when you break your subconscious pattern, new options have the chance to emerge.

So remember...

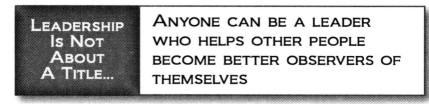

LEADERSHIP IS NOT ABOUT A TITLE...

ANYONE CAN BE A LEADER WHO HELPS OTHER PEOPLE BECOME BETTER OBSERVERS OF THEMSELVES

Practice #11—Take Your Oxygen Daily

Occasionally I lose it. I remember one time when my life had been really stressful over several months. I won't delve into details, except for this: I had just spent an inordinate amount of time creating new program materials and establishing new client relationships in a non-stop series of events, culminating in three straight weeks of my being "on stage" every day, including several evenings and off-shifts and long travel days. All of this was going on while I was also managing three long-term projects and the usual comings and goings in my personal life, including successive, frenzied, no-time-to-sit-down weekends and numerous personal and family transitions (like children moving out and moving in, addressing some minor health issues, and putting in a new lawn!). Hmm, I just realized that I am getting tied up in knots just thinking about the wild spin I'd worked myself into!

Have you ever had a time like that in your life? In the midst of the spinning, I began to feel vaguely disoriented, but kept telling myself, "Life is good! Business is good! I'm making lots of progress! Everything's under control!" So, I showed up in a conversation with my coach, and I kept telling him about all the stuff I was doing, and how great things were, and he said something that stopped me dead in my tracks:

"Jim, I think you're burning out."

"What? No way! <pause> Uh. Well. Hmmm. <pause> You know what? That sounds... actually... <pause> that sounds right."

I was a boiled frog. I was sitting in a pot of water about to boil, and I was so focused on BUSY that I'd stopped paying attention to taking care of myself. That "vague disorientation" I felt was my system about to collapse on itself.

My coach's observation shifted my awareness from what I was *doing* to how I was *being*. And once I accepted the word 'burnout' as possibly true, I started to notice all the other things that were going on for me. I had not slept well for a couple weeks. My caffeine intake had spiked. My temper was on a short fuse. I was, when I stopped to notice, feeling physically phffft—if I stopped moving for more than a few minutes, I started to fall asleep.

Amazing, isn't it, how well we can ignore our body's signals when we are involved in something else? The good news was that I did not have to start from scratch in creating actions to pull myself back into a lower stress mode. I did, however, have to pay attention to what was (not) happening with my daily oxygen practices.

~~☺~~☺~~☺~~☺~~

Daily Oxygen Practices

Many years ago I figured out that, as a visual learner, I feel more motivated to exercise when I track my progress on a chart. Then about four years ago I expanded my tracking to include ALL the things I do to take care of myself, which includes cardio and/or resistance exercise, yoga, meditation, deep breathing, and journaling (I do not, despite rumor, track my dark chocolate consumption).

I call these my Daily Oxygen Practices. The terminology comes from my Happiness Foundation #1: Take Your Own Oxygen First, which itself derives from the pre-flight talk in which flight attendants show us how to exit the plane, connect our seat belt, and put on an oxygen mask, with the instruction, *"If you are traveling with someone who needs assistance, put on your own oxygen mask, first!"*

Oxygen is the fuel of life. And if I'm on empty, I'm not much good to anyone else, am I? When I looked at my oxygen-tracking chart, I was shocked. Without conscious awareness, I'd dropped from my usual 6–7 days a week of Daily Oxygen Practices to just twice a week over the prior month. I was taking in a small amount of oxygen; I was also using it up faster than normal. I was darn close to empty.

The fabulous thing about awareness is that, though it's the hardest part, taking action is easy once we are aware of the need. I am often reminded of the mantra I learned in my early career: "a problem well-defined is 90% solved." In other words, problems are easy to solve, once you have identified the CORRECT problem.

We spend a lot of our time addressing symptoms. For example, when we feel out of shape, we look for a quick diet to fix our waistline for vacation rather than changing our lifestyle to live differently. In this case, I was in anxiety, and could have gone to my doctor to get a sedative for the short term. But the core issue is lack of oxygen. This I can address on my own. Once my awareness shifted, I stopped letting myself "get away with" cheating on myself. I'm back to starting each day with a short meditation, to making sure I get my body moving for at least 30 minutes every day, and I am feeling SO MUCH BETTER!

The stressors still exist—yet they are not dragging me down. My oxygen levels are back to normal.

Applying the Skill: Create your own Daily Oxygen Practice list. You can do it in just a few minutes.

1. What feeds your soul? What are the activities that put oxygen back into your tank or help restore balance to your life?
2. Your oxygen-fueling activities might be daily or weekly (e.g. one of my weekly practices is attending Mass at my church).
3. You might consider these areas: Work, Personal/Health, Relationships/ Family, and Creativity (optional).
4. List no more than 2–3 activities in each area. These are the activities that you know rejuvenate you and bring you back into balance.
5. Post the list where you'll see it or can access it regularly.
6. Whenever you feel yourself feeling stressed or like you're running out of oxygen, check the list. Notice if you've been ignoring one of your priorities, and then act on it to refuel yourself.

The very act of listing your own Daily Oxygen Practices can feel like an oxygen-infusing event. When you take care of you first, you build your capacity to show up for all the others in your life who depend on you. Best of all, you support your own Happiness!

~~☺~~☺~~☺~~☺~~

Refueling For The Future

I came of age in the corporate world working for a company that lived according to a "work hard, play hard" philosophy. The company had a (well-deserved) reputation as a white-collar sweatshop; the pressure to perform was relentless, the standards impossibly high, and the competition intense. The company was filled with high-achievers who worked long hours to support growth that often exceeded 25% per year for a decade. It was brutal.

AND we knew how to party like crazy! Once a year the company virtually shut down for a Halloween competition that was absolutely insane, with complete sets built in the cubicle villages as a backdrop for costume creativity that was simply over the top. Project completion events were often blowout affairs with music, dancing, and recognition ceremonies that resembled the Academy Awards. Even mundane "backlog parties" might involve every level of the department and require truckloads of pizza and a festive theme. In other words, even as people were working incredibly hard, the backdrop was about enjoying the work, recognizing contribution, and encouraging people to have fun and express their creativity.

Every culture is different, of course. In many organizations the same outcomes can occur through quiet conversation and low-key recognition. What's key is that some form of renewal and recognition do occur on a regular basis.

When we take time to celebrate accomplishments, give recognition for jobs well done, provide flexibility for personal lives, and occasionally have (gasp!) FUN at work, we put fuel into the tanks of all employees. That fuel provides the energy for those individuals—and thus the team—to keep moving fast into the future.

What are the oxygen-fueling practices in your organization? OR, are you—or the culture—"too busy" to take time for people? Be aware that if you do not deliberately take time every so often to attend to the (mental, emotional, and physical) health of your team members, you may find that stress and burnout spread quickly.

So remember...

LEADERSHIP IS NOT ABOUT A TITLE...	ANYONE CAN BE A LEADER WHO MAKES REFUELING AND FUN SERIOUS WORKPLACE PRIORITIES

Dirty Happy

I find happiness in the dirtiest places. Really! I absolutely LOVE working outside in the yard. I like mowing the lawn, weeding flower beds, pruning, trimming, edging, and fertilizing. I get excited when I fill my compost bin in the fall and then open it weeks later to find the composting insects have reduced all that yard waste to healthy organic humus that, when added to a garden, makes things grow tall and strong. Most of all, I love Spring, when the world is awash in lush greens and brilliant splashes of yellow, purple, pink, white, and red after months of winter grey. I'm constantly rearranging the landscape in our yard, and in springtime I can yank things out of the ground, rip them apart, pop them back into a new home and watch them grow beautifully. Nature is totally forgiving in the Spring—it's all about life and birth and beginnings.

Not long ago I spent two weekends digging, clipping, and rearranging things; erected new landscaping, and planted and mulched over 150 new perennials and flowering annuals in my yard, my mom's yard, and at my daughter's house.

My back ached, my knee throbbed from a nasty encounter with a large root, and it took me over a week to dig the dirt from under my fingernails. And it felt great—my oxygen tank was on full!

Practice #12—Practice The Skill Of Savoring

Have you ever had an experience that was so positive and powerful that you wanted it to last forever? Did you find yourself basking in the moment, soaking it in, noticing every aspect of the moment? Did you feel like you could not wait to tell others about it? Did you bring your pictures, and tell your story to an eager audience, reliving the experience over and again? If you answer "yes" to any of the above, you have engaged in the skill of Savoring. Savoring is a powerful way to build your positive emotion (aka happiness) muscle. Savoring is the conscious act of slowing down to notice and enjoy a part of life.

What happens when we use the skill of savoring? We fill up our own tank for the next part of the trip. We create a tool (memory) we can use at a future low point to pull us back up. We can even spread our good feelings to others thru sharing.

In the Afterword of this book you will find a story about how I applied the skill of Savoring to help others and myself in a very difficult time. Meanwhile, here are four techniques for building your "positive emotion muscles" using the skill of Savoring:

Absorption: slowing down in the moment, and noticing all the sensations you are experiencing. Immerse yourself totally in what is happening. Eat a bowl of popcorn one kernel at a time, noticing the sweet/salt taste on your tongue and the feel of it in your mouth; resist the urge to just shovel it in. Go to a movie or a play and completely let go of your reality; flow with the film as though you were in it yourself. Attend a family event and allow yourself to let go of everything outside while you soak in every little detail and nuance—the smile on Mom's face, the joyful play of your two-year old nephew, the happy chaos (or quiet togetherness) of interaction that you normally take for granted.

Memory-Building: the act of creating mementoes of a moment. Memory building occurs when we take pictures, buy souvenirs on vacation, do scrap booking, or attach a sound or sensation to an event. Do certain songs bring back good memories of your teen years, a certain person, a special time or event in your life? It happens all the time; you can intentionally create positive memories when you focus on this skill.

Self-Appreciation/Self-Congratulation: is about giving yourself permission for POSITIVE self-talk. It's saying to yourself, "I am so proud of you. I think you did a great job!"

Sharing: occurs when we tell our own vacation stories or relive with a friend how her boyfriend surprised her with a marriage proposal over the weekend. Telling others our "story" as a way to relive an experience is the most powerful way of savoring.

~~☺~~☺~~☺~~☺~~

One Wedding And A Thousand Memories

After 18 months of anticipation and planning, my daughter Kelly's wedding finally occurred. Even weeks later, my head was still spinning as I processed it all. Savoring a good memory is a very powerful way to experience positive emotions for you, and storytelling is a means to share positive emotions with others. So if you don't mind, I'm going to share some random wedding memories as a means of spreading some happiness!

This phrase kept running thru my head the entire week after the wedding: I cannot recall a time in my life when, in a single day, I laughed so much, hugged so many people, cried so often, expressed thanks so many times, loved my family so completely, and danced so much and for so long. Especially the dancing part. ☺ I found myself constantly surprised by the little things that, for me, made the day almost magical:

The place: On Thursday before the wedding, we arrived in South Bend, where the wedding took place, to attend to a myriad of details, including a final meeting with the hotel staff regarding logistics—and we got our first look at the hall, which had been undergoing a major renovation when we last saw it. I've seen many pretty banquet halls before, yet the first sight of this one absolutely took my breath away—because this one was for MY daughter's wedding. The head table, lit from underneath by a thousand tiny white lights, hovered above a sea of white—white chairs, white tables, white china—all set in a ballroom done in shades of cream and yellow. For me, breathtaking.

The planner: The final meeting with the wedding coordinator at the Basilica at Notre Dame, who kept emphasizing to Kelly, "this is your wedding. However you want it to be, just tell me." Her job, she reminded us, is essentially Stage Manager: to ensure that every detail—on stage and behind the scenes—happens as it should. And I thought, "Wow, what a cool job." Every week she manages two Perfect Weddings. Hers is a happy-making job, for sure!

The forgotten: Midori, the mother of the groom, flying in from Seattle, WA, forgot her suitcase at home with all her clothes—oops. Fortunately, at the last minute, she'd put her wedding-day dress in Mark's suitcase because he had extra room. Whew! Disaster averted. Everything else was taken care of in a couple hours at the mall with an overheated Visa card!

The groom himself, meanwhile, realized he'd forgotten the wedding rings at home in Cleveland (like mother, like son?!). This little oops a Visa card could not fix! However, a neighbor in Cleveland with a key helped my brother-in-law retrieve the rings, and they arrived on Friday in time for the rehearsal.

How beautiful the mother of the bride looked in her dress. It was an appropriately modest, mother-of-the-bride dress; at the same time, it was the first article of clothing Cheryl's ever owned that was custom-made for her. The dress fit her like a glove, and she looked incredibly graceful and elegant.

The degree of calm Kelly demonstrated throughout the day. Even in the midst of "the bobby-pin crisis" (her veil came loose 10-minutes prior to the ceremony!), she was relaxed and enjoying her day. A moment: Kelly, her mother, and I doing yoga breathing together in the rear of the church as the processional music began. In… out… calm….

Charlie Weis, the Notre Dame head football coach, was attending a fund-raising event elsewhere in the hotel. When he learned there was "Notre Dame wedding" going on in the grand ballroom, he came down to congratulate the bride and groom—who coincidentally were hanging out with their photographer at the hall entrance. They were thrilled to have a photo taken with Charlie (a moment, perhaps, that only Fighting Irish fans can truly appreciate!).

The geographic spread of the guest list. The 175 people who attended came from three continents (friends from Ireland and Paul's grandmother from Japan) and from 16 states in the U.S. This truly was a wedding of Millennials.

The symbolism: At one point in the wedding planning, there was a long family discussion over who would walk Kelly down the aisle. Depending on where you stood, it was part conversation, part controversy. Nevertheless, it is a key moment in the ceremony and we all wanted to get it right. So here's how we finally resolved it. Cheryl and I walked with Kelly from the foyer halfway up the basilica. There we stopped and gave her a kiss, then took the cross-aisle path to the outside pews and arrived at our seats in time to see her process up the center aisle on her own to meet Paul at the front of the church. This symbolic act made everyone happy—Cheryl and I have BOTH played a part in Kelly's life, but we've only taken her partway. She's on her own now, and meets Paul not as someone who's being "given away," but on her own and as his equal. It was actually pretty cool.

Raw emotional moments. Paul is a very calm and easy-going guy, so it was quite a surprise to see him overcome with emotion as Kelly came up the aisle. When it came time for the vows, Paul was at first unable to speak, and that gave the entire ceremony a much deeper meaning, I thought. He is so completely and deeply in love with Kelly!

Finally, *how much FUN I had*! I've been to lots of weddings in my life, but this was the first wedding that we've ever *hosted*. There are not enough words to express how fabulous it felt to be surrounded by all the people we love and care about and who love us and care about us. It was simply the most joyous thing I've ever done. Joy, happiness, tiny spurts of panic, contentment, calm, concern, appreciation, zest, enthusiasm, excitement, gratitude, connectedness, reunion, friendship, support, pride… what an emotional feast!

Afterword: Using Happiness Skills In Terrible Times

Personal Reflection: Savoring Kara

Monday morning, September 27, 2004, dawned warm, dry, and sunny. After my morning walk I settled into what was scheduled to be a full day of coaching. At 10:10 AM, as I was wrapping up my third client of the morning, my doorbell rang. I looked out and saw a police car in my driveway. "Hang on," I told my client. "There's a police officer at my door—probably something with the neighbor" (whose house was currently empty as she was in the hospital). When I saw the officer's face, however, I started to worry.

"Your daughter's been in an accident."

"Is it serious?"

"Yes, it's serious. You need to contact Shirley at Akron City Hospital."

"HOW serious? Why didn't they just call me?"

"You need to contact Shirley, immediately."

Over the next few minutes my world spun dizzily. "Randy? I have to end our call. I'll let you know later." "Hello? Can I speak with Shirley? Can't you tell me anything more than 'it's serious?' What does that mean? Yes, of course—we'll come right away." "Cheryl, Kara's been in an accident. No, they won't tell me much. You need to come home right away. I'm clearing my schedule and I'll be ready when you arrive. Hurry!" And the phone conversations with my clients went on for several surreal minutes as I cleared my schedule while waiting for Cheryl...

The 30-minute drive took five minutes and it took five hours. Spinning out of control, time seemed to flow incredibly fast and yet not at all. When we pulled into the Emergency Bay at the hospital to ask where to park, the officer on duty looked right at us and said, "Mr. and Mrs. Smith? You can park right here." I remember a chill went through me. How did he know who we were?

** Like a Scene from *E.R.* **

We were ushered into a private room to wait. A clerk stopped by to complete admissions paperwork. We were offered coffee, water, and a telephone. Shortly, a doctor and nurse joined us. I remember thinking, in a disconnected way, that the nurse looked as though she had been crying. The scene was right out of an "E.R." script:

"Your daughter was barely breathing when the paramedics brought her in. We worked on her for a long time, but despite our best efforts... ."

"What do you mean, unable to revive her? Do you mean…?"

"Yes."

At that point time stopped entirely—I only remember pieces of the conversation after that:

"We believe it was a hemorrhage in her brain… it's difficult even for us to believe… she does not have a mark on her body… the air bag deployed… there is no sign of trauma… she is quite beautiful… we are so sorry for your loss."

** "We are so sorry for your loss." **

I was to hear those words over and again for the next six days. [Weeks later, after the accident investigators and medical examiner turned in their reports, we learned that Kara had not died as a result of the accident, but rather the accident had been a result of her death. When the aneurysm in her brain burst, she likely lost consciousness immediately. At the time, she was driving to school on the highway. Her car kept going, bouncing right and then left, across four lanes of rush-hour congestion before it hit the median. Miraculously, no one else was hurt].

Our 22-year-old daughter, who believed in guardian angels so much that she chose Angela for her confirmation name, was suddenly an angel herself. Our little Asian Beauty, whom we adopted from Thailand when she was 9-years old and who had been such an important part of our lives for 13 years, was gone. Left behind: mom, dad, older sister, and two younger brothers.

This is the sad part of my story. The rest is about what goodness emerged. Within hours, everyone knew. And in the next five days we learned as much about Kara as we thought we already knew. Hundreds and hundreds and again hundreds of people came to the wake service. And at least half of them said to us, "Kara was my good friend." People she knew from grade school, high school, college, her place of work for four years, and from her life.

** "Kara was my good friend." **

We learned about what an amazing person she was. We laughed at new stories, and stood in awe of the immense amount of love that people held for her. Former schoolteachers told of the special regard they held for the little girl who struggled with English but excelled on the soccer field. Girlfriends who had been her "special buddy" in the second grade when she spoke not a word of English, told us of their special bond and that, "I will always remember her." And in this Internet-era funeral for a Net-Generation child, nearly 100 people posted web logs to Kara's online obituary—happy memories of her along with messages of support, sympathy, love, and hope for us.

How does this tie to Happiness? Throughout the week, even as I grieved for Kara, I also marveled at the strength and resilience of our friends and family. I noticed how a great many people—myself included—were able to hold, almost simultaneously, grief over her death and a celebration of her life;

sadness for her absence, yet gratitude that she had, however improbably from halfway around the world, passed our way.

Cheryl and I, even in the midst of our grieving, found happiness in the fact that we had no regrets. When Kara had last been at the house three days before her death, we'd parted on good terms, with hugs and "I love yous" all around. When she died, we were "whole" with each other. We found some peace and joy and comfort in that fact.

** Savoring Kara **

I was determined to deliver a eulogy at Kara's funeral. I turned to the tool of Savoring to assemble that eulogy. I contacted many people from her life—her boyfriend, close friends, and family—and asked them to share a story or a memory of Kara with me. I wove what they gave me into the memorial I shared with the more than 400 people who attended her funeral mass. If you'd like to learn more about Kara, you can read her eulogy.
http://www.TheExecutiveHappinessCoach.com/happiness/eulogy.cfm

That act of sharing, of Savoring, her life had a most amazing and calming effect on me and those who had helped me write the eulogy. I believe that sharing Kara's story with others has ensured that in some small way, she is still present with us—in our hearts, in our memories, and in our love. And for that, I will always be happy.

** Happiness is not just for the "good times" **

I am fairly certain that some readers may be thinking it odd that I chose to speak of such sadness in a book about Happiness. Why? Because this tragic event helped me to realize, on a very deep level, that *The 13 Principles of Happiness* and the tools of *positive emotion* are not just for enhancing the good times in life. Indeed, it is during the bad times that we most have need of the strength and resilience that come from the intentional use of Gratitude, Forgiveness, Joy, Happiness, Calm, Optimism, and—above all—Hope.

Thank you for allowing me to share this story. I appreciate the chance to savor, once more, Kara's memory.

Kara Watsana Angela Smith
b. 1982, Chang Mai Province, Thailand
d. 2004, Cleveland, Ohio, USA.

In Happiness, J.

A Question... And A Challenge:

In what ways might you make intentional use of the tools of Happiness today to increase your resilience tomorrow?

Footnote to Loss: Creating a New Normal

If you have experienced a deep loss in your life, I extend to you my heartfelt sympathies. And I'd like to offer you a tool that helped my family to come back from a dark and terrible place.

Several weeks after Kara's funeral, Cheryl and I visited the cemetery to select a vault where Kara's ashes were to be interred. The woman who escorted us around the grounds shared a common bond—her son had died suddenly at age 21. We asked her how she and her husband had coped.

"People kept telling us that things would eventually get back to normal," she said. "But we realized that would never happen. Our world was changed forever. So we decided to create a New Normal." Hmm. This concept really stuck with Cheryl and I.

When Thanksgiving arrived just six weeks after the funeral, we felt too much sadness to bring everyone to our home. So we went on the road and had our turkey dinner at my daughter's apartment in Philadelphia. We never have Thanksgiving dinner on a Thursday any more. New Normal.

We carefully examined all our holiday obligations and traditions and made deliberate decisions to end some and to change others. We established new boundaries with family and learned to feel comfortable saying No when we felt the situation would create stress for us. New Normal.

At Christmas time we considered retiring the angel that Kara had always placed on top of the tree; instead, we used ceramic paints to convert the blond angel to a black-haired, Asian angel. New Normal.

Before, we'd always said to people, "We have four children." Now, what do we say? "We have three kids?" That felt disrespectful to Kara. "Our younger daughter died?" Ugh, why open every conversation with sadness? After much consideration, we changed our story to: "We *raised* four children." A small shift in our language that felt exactly right to us. New Normal.

Creating a New Normal gave us the courage and the language to examine our lives and to explain to family and friends why we were—or were not—making changes in our life. New Normal gave us the strength to recover from loss, because we had permission to not have to ever get back to "the way things were."

New Normal helped our family build our future. If the concept can help in your own situation, then we feel blessed to share it with you.

~~☺~~☺~~☺~~☺~~

Acknowledgements

I feel an immense sense of gratitude to all who supported me on the journey of creation:

- Cheryl Ann Smith, my life partner, who has always believed in me, even when I did not.

- My children, Kelly, Kara (RIP), Justin, and Jared, who endured my learning, were my first guinea pigs for applying what I learned about Attitude, and who apparently absorbed a lot more Happiness growing up than I ever thought possible.

- Elaine Eichman, who first invited me to deliver a speech on Happiness because "you're always talking about it, Jim!" I never imagined that the challenge to create a one-time fun program for a roomful of over-stressed blood bank managers would eventually transform my world.

- Rob Berkley, MCC, who coached me through a Vision Day® process that led to my reincarnation as The Executive Happiness Coach®.

- Sherry Greenleaf, who was the first friend with enough guts to show me my own incompetence… thus inspiring the learning journey that I've been on since.

- Michelle James, founder of CreativeEmergence.com, who always helps me remember that I am whole, creative, and resourceful.

- Martin Seligman, PhD, the father of Positive Psychology, who opened up a whole new world of possibility for me when he merged Happiness and Science and led the Authentic Happiness Coach program in 2003.

- All the readers of my newsletter, *Happiness @TheSpeedofLife,* who have stayed in the happiness conversation with me since 2002.

- All those who encouraged me, nagged me, insisted I had a book in me, and served as readers, proofers, contributors, and cheerleaders along the way. The world is a happier place because of good friends!

—Appendix: Web Resources—

All the sites in the order they appear in the book in one place. Go surf the Internet.

URLs and notes

- www.TheExecutiveHappinessCoach.com —The author's website

- http://tinyurl.com/Happiness13 —For a full-color copy of *The 13 Principles of Happiness* suitable for framing or posting

- http://www.authentichappiness.com —Authentic Happiness website. Register to create an account, and then explore the many tools and assessments in the Testing Center.

- http://www.theexecutivehappinesscoach.com/resources/values.pdf —An exercise to help you identify and prioritize your personal Core Values

- http://corporate.ritzcarlton.com/en/About/GoldStandards.htm —To take a look at the Ritz Carlton Credo

- http://www.despair.com/indem.html —Take your sense of humor with you when you visit the Despair.com site, and remember that three seconds of laughter is equal to three minutes of aerobic exercise!

- http://www.youtube.com/watch?v=tkzr0naZnZ0 —The award-winning Honda Commercial featuring one of the coolest Rube Goldberg machines ever created.

- www.TheEvolutionofDance.com —Comedian Judson Laipply's classic YouTube video. Turn up the volume and have fun!

- www.hellomynameisscott.com —Scott Ginsberg has worn a nametag 24/7 since Fall 2000, turning it into a brand and his business. He is an expert on approachability.

- http://www.eepybird.com/dcm1.html —Mentos and Diet Coke Experiment 137. If you like it, explore the other experiments.

- www.yesand.com —A portal into the world of improv and creativity

- www.CreativeEmergence.com —Another resource on Improv and Creativity

- http://acomplaintfreeworld.org/ —To order A Complaint Free World wristbands or learn how to use them as you seek to go 21 days without complaining. Simple, not easy.

- http://www.emergingleader.com/article21.shtml —For an overview of Mastermind Groups.

- http://www.creativityatwork.com/articlesContent/playwork.htm —A tips list for creating Play at Work

- **http://tinyurl.com/GatesTalk** —Bill Gates on using technology to improve people's lives. He is a leader who cares.

- www.Tut.com —Sign up to receive a daily inspirational "Message from the Universe"

- http://www.eliterunners.com —Home of my brother's business, Elite Runners and Walkers, selling high-quality shoes and running gear to professional & recreational runners and a huge fund raiser for Team In Training

- http://www.NewfieldNetwork.com —A wonderful learning community for coaching, personal transformation, and creating change in the world.

- www.TheExecutiveHappinessCoach.com/happiness/eulogy.cfm —the eulogy I delivered at Kara's funeral in 2004.

- www.TheExecutiveHappinessCoach.com —Subscribe to the monthly coaching newsletter, Happiness @TheSpeedofLife, to continue your happiness journey

- www.LifeWithHappiness.com —Join the ongoing conversation on Happiness at Jim's blog

ENDNOTES

1. Compton, William C. *An Introduction to Positive Psychology*. Wadsworth Publishing (2005), 1-22.

2. Snowden, David, et al. "The Nun Study." http://www.mc.uky.edu/nunnet/

3. For more on the nature of Improv: Improvise This: A Revolutionary Technique *For Achieving Dramatic Results In Business And In Life*, by Mark Bergren, Molly Cox, and Jim Detmar (Hyperion, 2002). Or, visit www.yesand.com, a wonderful portal into the world of improv and creativity.

4. DeBono, Edward. *Six Thinking Hats*. Back Bay Books (1999). The Six Thinking Hats were also introduced in *Teach Your Child How To Think*, Viking, 1993. This latter book was responsible for an enormous shift in the way my wife and I raised our children, most especially after we adopted our daughter, Kara Watsana, from Thailand. Raised in an institutional environment from age 3 to 9, she lacked many foundational skills. My dog-eared copy of DeBono's book was a reference for us as we strove to teach Kara—and all our children—the skills of lateral and creative thinking. Moving these skills into the workplace was a natural progression for me, and coworkers at several companies learned how to use the Six Thinking Hats through my bringing them into the conversation. The tools work!

5. Even if you are not into analyzing energy flow or baguas, Kingston's book will provide you with a wealth of practical tips to help simplify your physical, mental, emotional, and spiritual environments, thus creating space for Happiness. *Clear Your Clutter With Feng Shui* is just one of several small, very readable books by this feng shui practitioner.

6. Many of these exercises are based in research—but I choose not to burden you with that. If you need such information, there are many fine books out there that will happily provide you details on the studies. From me, you'll get the practice and the coaching to (with all due respect to Nike) Just Do It and notice for yourself how it works!

7. Snyder C. R., and Shane J Lopez. *Positive Psychology: The Scientific and Practical Explorations of Human Strengths*. Sage Publications, Inc. (2006)

Continue your Happiness journey. Get more!

Since 2002 Jim has published an e-newsletter to provide tips and tools for the practice of Happiness and positive emotional experience in your life and your workplace.

To subscribe to this monthly coaching newsletter, visit www.TheExecutiveHappinessCoach.com

or email Jim at

happiness-ezine@aweber.com

And remember:

Happiness is a Decision, not an Event!